21 Reasons for Trusting in God

Finding Inner Peace in His Existence

By L.A. Buckley

Contents

Introduction

How did I get here? What is the purpose of my existence? Am I significant? And if so, what is this worth based on? You may wonder if there is a solid answer to these questions that is grounded in truth. Pondering life leads to one of the most fundamental questions in human experience - Is God real?

If you're a young adult stepping out into the world and beginning your search for truth, there is no doubt this is a question you have asked yourself. Perhaps you are the parent of a young adult or a teen. If this is the case, you may be trying to respond to your child's questions about God. Whatever the case, it's important to remember that the answer shapes every aspect of our lives, who we become, and ultimately our eternity.

Even if you're convinced God does exist, you probably wonder how you can be sure. What are the reasons for trusting in God? In a world of so many different belief systems, it may seem absurd to claim that faith in Jesus Christ is the only way to Heaven, and that the Bible is, without fail, the word of God. Why not the Quran and Islam? Why not Buddhism and the Tripitaka? Why the Bible and Jesus Christ?

I want to assure you God is real. The Bible is His word. Jesus died for your sins. He loves you more than you can ever imagine and is worth your trust.

What's even more astonishing is He is a perfect and loving God. He does not leave us to our own devices to determine His existence. After all, it would be cruel for Him to make it impossible for us to tell if He is there, especially if He desires that we trust Him. Nature should point to a creator; history should align with the timeline of the Bible; and philosophy and morality should point toward a loving and perfect God.

As you read this book, your eyes will be opened to the incredible beauty of how God has worked Himself into all these things. Jesus is more than a historical figure but the Son of God who died for our sins.

With so much science explaining the natural world and discoveries continuing to be made, is God still relevant in explaining the origins of the universe? In simple words, does science disprove God?

The answer is no. God is very relevant to what is going on in the world today. While science is incredible and has opened our eyes to many things, it has yet to answer all of our questions. After all, we have yet to discover how life began, how human consciousness arose, and why the universe is so complex and precise. Such an organization points to an intelligent designer or Creator.

Based on this, it's important to remember that science and faith in a Creator don't have to be mutually exclusive. It doesn't have to be one or the other. For example, it does not have to be that every aspect of evolution is true and God doesn't exist or that no part of evolution is true and God does exist. Science and God work together. What science doesn't explain, faith in a Creator does explain. The end of science is where God begins.

These are big things to contemplate. They can feel overwhelming and impossible to unravel in our limited human experience. Let me be the first to assure you that feeling is perfectly normal, and no, it's not impossible to grasp the answers.

Questioning doesn't necessarily have to lead to doubt; an honest look at more profound questions can lead to a stronger faith. God loves us so much that He is gracious enough to meet us where we are. It is healthy to search for answers to our difficult questions prayerfully. Many practical questions cause believers some doubt and confusion. I wrote this book to help people understand why we should believe. For example:

1. **How can I fully trust God when I can't physically see or touch Him?**

2. **What happens after death? Do Heaven and hell really exist?**

3. **What should I trust? Scientific evolution or creation?**

4. **If God is real, then why do people suffer?**

Ultimately, honest and reasonable questions like these led you to buy this book. You want to see how God's existence relates to your own beliefs and life experiences.

As you form your identity outside of the environment you grew up in, you will be exposed to a whole range of new worldviews. You may have doubts about being a Christian and about the story presented in the Bible. This book will give you a solid basis to move forward. It is for all who seek God. My heart behind it is that it will help you in your journey to find the truth.

I'm a believer in Christ who has wrestled with the same doubts and questions as you. One of my most profound reasons for believing is that I have seen the Lord work miracles in my life. I've been blessed with an exemplary family background, with many family members serving in ministry. As a mother, my scientific-minded teen told me he no longer believed in God. We were able to have an open conversation. Eventually, I was able to provide him with the evidence needed for him to have confidence that God is real.

My journey of faith has taught me lessons and given me spiritual insights. I want to share the knowledge I've gained with you. The knowledge that will make talking to your teen easier. The knowledge that will help you believe. For those seeking the truth, information such as this should be accessible and easy to find.

I'm not the one who discovered all the practical historical, theological, and philosophical evidence I am sharing with you. This evidence results from the combined efforts of truth seekers like yourself, who experienced their own journey of faith to find the answers.

CHAPTER 1

Science and the Existence of God

Wondering whether God exists may be an unsettling thought process, and you are not alone. The philosopher Spinoza asked the same questions as far back as the mid-1600s. He concluded that *"God is everywhere, and everything that exists is a modification of God. Human beings know God through only two of his attributes— thought and extension (the quality of having spatial dimensions) — though the number of God's attributes is infinite."* (Baruch Spinoza from Britannica)

Two centuries later, Albert Einstein, a theoretical physicist, responded to a Rabbi in New York when questioned if he believed in God by saying, *"I believe in Spinoza's God, who reveals himself in the orderly harmony of what exists, not in a God who concerns himself with the fates and actions of human beings."* (Interview with Einstein conducted by G.S. Viereck and published in the October 26, 1929 edition of The Saturday Evening Post.)

Science has come a long way in recent years. As a result, we have learned more about our world and universe, including its creation. Still, many brilliant people, including scientists, philosophers, and historians, have concluded that there is a

God, while others disagree. The debate goes back and forth like a tennis ball between players.

Questioning your beliefs is important. It is crucial to seek answers for yourself. Two fundamental questions:

Is there a God?

Does He concern Himself with the universe and with you and me?

By the way, Spinoza was later excommunicated from his synagogue, although it is unclear whether his view on God was responsible. Perhaps you can identify with him holding a widely unpopular view with your peers. Maybe you've never given God much thought or are exploring your views and opinions. Let's examine some of the scientific reasons to believe.

Reason #1: Science Points to a Creator

Science and faith seem to conflict with one another. Or do they? You may think you must choose one or the other: science or faith.

Take DNA (deoxyribonucleic acid), for example. DNA is present in every cell. It has no other purpose but to transmit genetic information, forming cells for its specific function. Billions of nucleotides make up the billions of atoms in a DNA molecule. The nucleic acids, adenine, cytosine, guanine, and thymine join in a specific order to form a unique code for each human cell. (There will be a test later!) Take an eye, for example; some cells group to create the iris with its unique color while other cells become light-sensitive retina cells. A set number of cells become part of the optic nerve that transmits electrical signals to the brain. The brain cells turn these signals into images so we can see.

Comparatively, Darwin's theory of evolution, or Naturalism, proposes that this complicated and intricately ordered genetic code sequence was assembled due to an explosive event. Can cell structure, DNA, be a random process through evolution?

This genetic code or blueprint for life is even more complicated than the most complex computer system. The code for DNA is 3 billion letters long. Each human being has a unique DNA code. This code can be used as evidence proving innocence or guilt in a court of law. Even in cold cases, when DNA is found and analyzed, the law regards the result of DNA testing as conclusive proof to convict a person.

So, where did the information in DNA come from? Darwinism or Naturalism fails to account for DNA. It holds that the information making up DNA spontaneously arose out of nowhere. Research says the probability of forming the DNA sequence by chance is *"7 trillion times smaller than the probability of finding a single specific atom in the entire universe of over 200 billion galaxies."* (Rooted-Blog. "Showing Teenagers How Science Points to God as Creator." *Rooted Ministry,* April 15, 2021)

The two concepts, science and faith, are not mutually exclusive. There is an intersection between the facts of science and the faith in a Creator. Science is a physical and tangible idea that can help us make sense of our world. However, the universe's beginning is the only case throughout recorded history of random, useful information being generated from a seemingly 'unexplained' source.

Personal Insights

Science and God are not in conflict. However, many struggle to align their belief in God with science. Looking into science for evidence is a worthwhile pursuit. It will help you see evidence of God's existence everywhere.

Understanding God's existence is not easy. I have been there too, and after searching for the truth, I can see the intersection of faith and science. They work together to show an intelligent, purposeful Creator who works His plan and design through science, not in conflict with it. Trusting in God helps me discover the beauty and complexity of our world.

God does not mind us having questions and doesn't expect us to believe unquestioningly. The Bible encourages us to search for evidence, *"Test all things; hold fast what is good."* (New King James Version, The Bible 1 Thessalonians 5:21)

Although we can't see God face-to-face, we can see His nature through the things He created. *"For since the creation of the world God's invisible qualities—his eternal power and divine nature—have been clearly seen, being understood from what has been made, so that people are without excuse."* (New International Version, The Bible, Romans 1:20)

Reason #2: Beyond the Big Bang

Scientists discuss the 'Big Bang' theory when explaining how the universe began. This term refers to a single point from which the cosmos, as we know it, expanded at excessive speed, heat, and density. Most of what we know about this theory has come from astronomers.

Data collected by the European Space Agency Planck Satellite produced an image of what has been named the Cosmic Microwave Background (CMB). The image shows an 'echo' of expansion. Through CMB mapping, science has proven that the universe has a starting point and has not always been here. The starting point was about 13.7 billion years ago. So, what caused this event? Nothing can come from nothing. There must be a cause – a catalyst behind every action – including the universe's beginning.

Time also plays into the beginning of the universe. Have you noticed that material objects never truly last? Everything that once functioned well breaks down over time. Every perfectly cleaned room becomes dirty once again. This concept of more disorder over time is called entropy. Entropy is defined as the world and everything in it continuously going from order to disorder, organization to chaos. The ultimate movement of energy over time is the same. It always goes from a state of being broken down to more disorder. Stephen Hawking, the theoretical physicist and cosmologist, states, *"The increase of disorder or entropy is what distinguishes the past from the future, giving a direction to time."* (A Brief History of Time, Stephen Hawking, 1988)

Time cannot be reversed. It is one-directional. Time flows forward with increasing entropy. Entropy, the second law of thermodynamics, also states that because all things progressively move toward disorder, all available energy needed for work will eventually be lost. If energy is constantly being used or redistributed, then at some point, all the energy in the universe will run out, and all movement will stop. But we know the universe is still running and functioning. Energy is being transferred, work is being performed, and as a result, life exists. We can see this in the world around us. Life and motion have not stopped.

Science has shown that the universe is finite. Since the universe is finite, it must have come into existence at a set point in time in the past. A force outside physical and natural laws sparked the universe into existence.

We know the universe had a beginning, but scientists have yet to show what or who the catalyst was. The Bible, the word of God, does not disprove science on this issue but increases our understanding. *"By faith, we understand that the worlds were framed by the word of God so that the things which are seen were not made of things which are visible. "* (The New King James Version, The Bible <u>Hebrews 11:3</u>)

Personal Insights

Whatever the triggering force behind the universe, it is greater than the universe, not subject to its laws, and outside of space and time. An obvious conclusion is a masterful designer set the stars, the planets — the entire universe in motion – 13.7 billion years ago. It makes sense that God was the cause, putting everything in motion.

The concept of an all-powerful, all-loving God existing outside of time and creating the universe can be overwhelming. The scientific evidence found in our universe gives reason to my belief. I understand why many believe in science and reasoning, and the concept of faith in God can be challenging to process. However, an honest and thorough look at science and reason undeniably points towards a God.

My friend shared a story of why she believes. When she was young, she worried her sins weren't forgiven. One night, my friend stood outside looking up at the night sky. She asked God to show her a shooting star if her sins were truly forgiven. Just then, a shooting star appeared out of nowhere. My friend felt peace and joy for many days because God sent her this sign. It wasn't the last time she worried about her sins being forgiven, but I know she still thinks of that night when God responded to her prayer for comfort and peace.

I don't think it is unreasonable to question God at times. I learn more about my relationship and His presence when I question His choices. God is constantly sending signs. Faith helps me recognize these signs.

"In the beginning, God created the Heavens and the Earth. The Earth was without form and void, and darkness was over the face of the deep. And the Spirit of God was hovering over the face of the waters. And God said, "Let there be light," and there was light. And God saw that the light was good. And God separated the light from the darkness. God called the light day and the darkness he called night. And there was evening, and there was morning, the first day." (English Standard Version, The Bible Genesis 1:1-31)

The Big Bang theory described or seen in the CMB by scientists only tells us so much: the scientific and material process by which the universe began, not what ultimately caused it to exist. Due to the lack of cause, many, over thousands of centuries, believe in a creator, God.

Reason #3: The Universe is Designed for Life

There is more to the universe than meets the eye. The conditions of the universe are perfect for supporting life. The universe's natural laws create the correct balance for us to thrive. Were these natural laws to fluctuate, even to the slightest degree, then we wouldn't exist. This principle is called fine-tuning. Fine-tuning is defined as "*a process in physics where the features of a system necessarily match or cancel out with such precision.*" (McRae, M. 2021, November 21. *Our Universe Is Finely Tuned for Life, and There's an Explanation for Why That Is So.* ScienceAlert)

The constants and quantities responsible for the order of our universe "happen" to fall perfectly within a specific range that allows for life and perfect balance. The possibility of this occurring without an outside force setting it in motion is infinitely small.

- Matter and energy are evenly distributed to support life.

- The sun is exactly the correct color to generate the strongest photosynthetic response.

- The Earth is at the perfect distance from the sun. If it were closer, the water on Earth would boil, or if it were further away, the water would freeze.

- The Earth's oxygen/nitrogen ratio is exact for supporting life.

As already mentioned, the universe's energy, or mass, and the expansion rate are so perfectly balanced that the universe continued to expand over the past 13.7 billion years. Another example of fine-tuning is that the number of protons and electrons are perfectly matched to produce a neutrally charged universe. If there were a few more electrons, the charge would be harmful, and the matter would push itself apart and into chaos.

These are only a fraction of the facts. There are many more examples of how the universe is finely tuned. Fine-tuning is one of the strongest arguments for an intelligent designer or Creator. It's improbable that such calculated exactness would result from the random chance of natural selection.

Where Faith is Reasonable

Science cannot give us physical or tangible evidence that the universe is the action of God, nor can science disprove it. When the evidence presented is thoroughly weighed and examined, it becomes evident that the universe couldn't have resulted from mere chance.

You don't need to abandon reason to embrace what science teaches. Science, Naturalism, and evolution cannot define how the universe was formed without an intelligent Creator. The reasonable answer is that God formed it. The intelligent design of the universe presents a plan and intention. It's finely-tuned and wonderfully complex, showing God set it up for life.

Personal Insights

The Bible tells us, "*We walk by faith and not by sight*" (English Standard Version, The Bible 2 Corinthians 5:7).

The Earth was created for man to inhabit. God is the reason behind the creation of the universe. We are humans with limited intellect. There is no way we can understand the mysteries of the universe on our own. Faith is necessary.

Though I cannot reach out and touch God, nor see Him with my eyes, I can see His beautiful creation. He created the universe intending to sustain life. We are made to love and to be loved.

Keep searching with an honest and sincere heart to know the truth. Keep an open mind, talk to God, and ask Him to reveal Himself through His creation. God is always listening and will reveal Himself to you if you sincerely look for Him. God will answer you. He reveals Himself to those who genuinely search for Him with an open and enquiring heart.

We are only at the beginning of our journey. In the next chapter, we will delve into the philosophical arguments that support the existence of God.

CHAPTER 2

Philosophical Arguments for God's Existence

You may have more questions now than when we started. That's okay because our discussion has only covered one aspect of the reasons for trusting God – Science. Some people prefer to make conclusions based on facts, while others are more interested in rational thought, discussion, and debate.

We now turn our attention to philosophical discussions. There are four broadly held philosophical arguments for God's existence: The ontological, cosmological, teleological, and moral arguments. Let's look at each of these.

Reason #4: Why God Must Exist

The ontological viewpoint was first suggested in 1078 by a monk named St. Anselm of Canterbury. He suggested, "If it's possible that God exists, then logically, it follows that God does exist."

The basis for this viewpoint stems from 'fine-tuning,' which we looked at in the previous chapter. As a recap, fine-tuning is how the universe's properties are so perfectly balanced that if one tiny detail were to be different, life could not exist as we know it.

St. Anselm begins by defining his premise's core term - God. St. Anselm described God as an incomparably great being. He starts with God as an essential and perfect being, or an incidental being.

Now, try to stay with me here. There is a second version of Anselm's ontological argument, including the premise that God is a being of incomparable greatness and dives into his original assumption that His existence is perfection. This variation states that a necessary existence is perfection. Anselm argues that a being of incomparable greatness whose existence is necessary or logically possible is more significant than a being whose existence is incidental or logically impossible. His argument further asserts that if there is nothing to contradict that God is an essential being, then He may exist as a necessary being.

If you can think of an entity to which nothing else is more significant, then you have a concept of God. Whether you believe God exists or not, we all have the same general idea when speaking of an incomparable significant entity. The ontological argument shows that if this singular, powerful entity exists in your mind and imagination, then by definition, you must think the incomparable great being also exists in reality.

About a century later, St. Thomas Aquinas, an Italian Priest, argued God's existence is self-evident and rejected the idea that a concept of God can simply be claimed into existence. In reference to Anselm's ontological viewpoint, St. Aquinas believed that even if we assume everyone shares the exact definition of God as a being of incomparable greatness, it does not automatically mean this being exists. St. Aquinas wants you and I to go beyond the ontological view of existence.

About five centuries later, Immanuel Kant, a philosopher, refuted all these theories by claiming that a being existing in the imagination of man and reality is more significant than a being that exists only as an idea in the mind. He argued that if something exists, it is a property and, therefore, greater than an imaginary being. So, how do we rectify these philosophical arguments?

Alvin Plantinga, a current-day analytical philosopher, gives a modal variation of the ontological argument. He states, "*If one says there is plausibly a God, then you are saying there is a plausible world in which God exists. Claiming that God necessarily exists is to say He exists in every plausible world. Therefore, God is necessarily perfect. Since God is necessarily perfect, he is perfect in every plausible world. If God is perfect in every plausible world, then he must exist in every plausible world and therefore exists. God is also essentially great; to be essentially great is to be perfect in every plausible world. So, it is possible that there is a God, and since God's existence is possible, then therefore He exists."* (Summarized from: The Internet Encyclopedia of Philosophy   https://iep.utm.edu/anselm-ontological-argument/#H4)

God's existence is philosophically supported. Thousands of people believe in and worship a greater being, God. According to the ontological argument, it's reasonable to conclude that the existence of a God is possible.

Personal Insights

The argument strives to support the existence of an incomparable great being. Those of us who believe in God agree He is an incomparable, greater being. In some ways, the definition mirrors God's nature. His goodness and enduring love are beyond this world. God is present everywhere, in our minds, hearts, and souls. At the same time, He has made Himself physically known, as found throughout the Bible, but most significantly with the birth of His son, Jesus.

In the Bible, we read:

"I am the Alpha and the Omega," says the Lord God, *"who is and who was and who is to come, the Almighty."* (English Standard Version, The Bible Revelation 1:8)

God said to Moses, *"I AM WHO I AM,"* and, *"Thus you shall say to the sons of Israel, 'I AM has sent me to you.'"* (English Standard Version, The Bible Exodus 3:14)

Both these Bible verses have an interesting parallel to the ontological argument. The first tells us how God is timeless throughout the past, present, and future. The latter defines God's existence by His own definition, "I AM WHO I AM."

Reason #5: The Universe Has a Beginning

Have you ever been on a walk at night and witnessed the majestic moonlight or seen the beauty of a shooting star? Have you wondered about the origins of the universe? If you have, you're not alone. Throughout millennia, humans have studied the universe. It's a natural curiosity that something inside us wants to know more about. God wants us to discover these mysteries.

The groundwork for the Cosmological argument is derived from these two questions:

1. Is the universe infinite? That is, nothing created it, but it has always been and always will be here.

2. Does the universe have a starting point? If so, is there a cause that brought it into existence, and is it reasonable to assume that the 'cause' was a mighty being or God?

A 12th Century Muslim philosopher named Al-Ghazali (full name Abū Ḥāmid Muḥammad ibn Muḥammad aṭ-Ṭūsiyy al-Ġazzālīy) first presented the Kalam Cosmological Argument. The argument is based on his statement: "*Every being which begins has a cause for its beginning; now the world is a being which begins; therefore, it possesses a cause for its beginning."*

The cosmological argument states the universe's existence is evidence of God's existence. The idea was adopted by Christian, Arab, Greek, and Jewish viewpoints for many centuries.

The three premises for this argument are:

1. Whatever begins to exist has a cause.

2. The universe began to exist.

3. Therefore, the universe has a cause for its beginning.

Let us take a closer look at each of the 3 points.

1. Whatever begins to exist has a cause: The first point in the Kalam Cosmological Argument is science, observation, and simple life experience show us that things do not randomly and spontaneously pop into existence without explanation. Events that occur must have a cause. For example, books do not materialize into reality randomly on your bookshelves. An author writes and prints them, and then they are bought or gifted.

William Lane Craig, a current-day analytical philosopher, defends this premise: *"It's not reasonable to claim that something came from nothing. If you sincerely believe that one thing comes from nothing, then everything must come from nothing. Since common experience and scientific evidence prove that things don't just appear from nothing, the fact that something cannot come from nothing is proved."* (Dr. Craig's 2015 lecture at the University of Birmingham on The Kalam Cosmological Argument)

2. <u>The universe began to exist</u>: Al-Ghazali's argument was based on the reasoning that if the universe never began to exist, then there must have been an infinite number of past events. However, he also held that infinite things cannot exist. Al-Ghazali asserted that a potentially unlimited number of things could exist but rejected the concept that an infinite number of things could exist. The term 'potentially infinite' is an ideal limit that can never be reached. He further believed that an infinite variation of improbabilities would result if an unlimited number of things could exist. To avoid these improbabilities, we must reject the concept that an actual infinite number of things exist. This implies that the universe cannot be without a beginning, so it began to exist.

3. <u>The universe has a cause for its beginning</u>: Every philosophical theory that claims the universe had a starting point must have an 'uncaused' cause within its reasoning, starting the chain of cause-and-effect events leading to the creation of the universe.

Empirical evidence in science and non-empirical theory in philosophy both point to the conclusion that the universe began to exist from a fixed starting point. Several empirical scientific studies also support the universe having a fixed starting point.

Here is a summarized list of a few key ones:

- *The second law of thermodynamics* determined that the universe is losing energy. It states that the universe is not infinite and has a set starting point. The universe would have run out of usable energy by now if it were infinite.

- *Albert Einstein's theory of relativity* gives us one of the first opportunities to discuss the past and the beginning of the universe. Things only have importance in relationship to other things. Later, scientists built on Einstein's equations and predicted that the universe expanded from a fixed point in time due to this relationship.

- *In 1929, Edwin Hubble measured light* from distant galaxies and made the same discovery that the beginning of the universe can be traced back to one fixed point in time. Hubble noticed that the light from distant galaxies was more red. This is known as the 'Red Shift.' The conclusion is the light waves are being stretched out as distant galaxies expand further from ours. The universe is still using energy, and by the law of thermodynamics, it cannot be infinite.

Personal Insights

I want to think I am here for a reason or cause. It's hard to imagine going through so much in this world only to die without an end purpose. We all search for a purpose in life. Otherwise, we would all be sitting on the couch doing nothing. Our natural inclination is to search for that purpose. For me, God fulfills that purpose.

If I believe God exists, my purpose or reason is to be with Him for eternity. It is better to believe and be wrong than not to believe at all! Besides, I don't want to find out God existed, not believe, and spend eternity in the underworld with Satan. I need and want the love of God to sustain me in my life, giving me an end cause for my existence.

Everyone's journey to discovering God is different. How you come to believe in Him isn't as important as the result.

The Bible tells us, "*All things came into being through Him, and apart from Him, nothing came into being that has come into being.*" (American Standard Version, The Bible John 1:3)

We cannot understand His nature. However, our hearts are designed to understand and receive His love. There is an emptiness in our hearts and our souls that only He can fill.

God is the cause of our existence.

"*In the beginning, God created the Heavens and the earth.*" (English Standard Version, The Bible Genesis 1:1)

Reason #6: How Design Points to a Designer

We discussed how science points to an intelligent designer from a scientific point of view. Let's look at this point from a philosophical point of view, the Teleological Argument.

Is there proof that God exists? The simple answer is yes and no.

Let me explain: If you want proof beyond a shadow of a doubt for use in a criminal court of law, then the answer is no. However, we are not dealing with that type of scenario. The argument we are examining here comes from an undisputed negative. We cannot prove that God doesn't exist; therefore, the existence of God is established by design. As discussed in the previous chapter, our world's concept, design, and intricate details require an intelligent designer.

The Law of Probability is applied when dealing with equally likely results. We can assume that if there is some evidence, such as global acceptance and historical events, then we can conclude that God exists.

Intelligent Design

Let's start by defining what we mean by 'intelligent design.' We are talking specifically about living things or wonders of the universe that another process, such as natural selection, cannot explain. This type of research usually involves scientists, philosophers, and academic scholars, all concurring that the exactness, intricacy, and perfect balance could not result from a random event.

Astrophysicist Hugh Ross gives an example in his book, The Creator and the Cosmos. *"In summary: The balance is so intricate that it is one part in 10^{37}. You can cover the entire North American continent with dimes, piling them up to the moon, a height of about 239,000 miles. Do the same on other continents of the same size. Imagine that amongst all these dimes, there is one red one. What are your odds of finding one red dime amongst all those others?"* (The Creator and the Cosmos, Hugh Ross, Edition 2001 pg. 150)

So, is intelligent design a delusion, or can we find some evidence or facts to support it?

The universe gives us evidence for an intelligent designer.

- A star can only remain in its place between two spiral arms in the sky at an exact distance from the galaxy center only if it orbits at the precise speed at which the arms rotate around the core.

- If the Earth were slightly bigger, hydrogen wouldn't escape gravity, and our world would be uninhabitable. If it were somewhat smaller, oxygen would be lost, and the water would evaporate, causing the same result - uninhabitable Earth.

- If the moon was smaller, the gravitational pull on the Earth would be effected causing a drastic change in climate, orbit and possible distruction of our planet!

- The planets each pivot at their own rate and at a different speed from Earth. If the Earth were at the same rotational speed as Jupiter, the wind on Earth would accelerate to such extremes that we would be blown away. Pivoting at the same speed as Venus would result in such long days that we would not survive the extreme heat on Earth.

- Humans need a precise concentration of 21% oxygen, and guess what? 21% is the exact concentration of oxygen in the Earth's atmosphere. If the concentration were higher, devastating fires would wipe us out.

- Astronomers say that if the Earth were placed just 2% differently from the sun, all the water would freeze permanently or evaporate based on the new location.

These are just a few constants we observe in the cosmos that show intricate detail and present the case for an intelligent designer. There are many more to discover and research.

Something extra to think about - according to the Oxford Dictionary, Creationism is the belief that the universe and all life began from a single act of Divine creation, as defined in the Bible. On the other hand, Evolutionists often refer to design in nature as 'an illusion of design,' refuting creationism. This standard counterargument to design is an attempt to explain that there is no need to assume there is a designer outside of the physical universe.

'Intelligent Design' does not set out to prove the premise of a designer but gathers facts and key geological and cosmological findings. These findings challenge other viewpoints that state our complex universe is a random process.

Personal Insights

The Bible tells us, "*For by Him, all things were created, in Heaven and on Earth, visible and invisible, whether thrones or dominions or rulers or authorities—all things were created through him and for him. And he is before all things, and in Him, all things hold together.*" (English Standard Version, The Bible Colossians 1:16-17)

Let me share a defining moment that pushed me into reaching for God and strengthened my faith in Him.

For 29 years, my husband, Steve, worked as a claims adjustor, spending a good portion of his time on the roofs of buildings. He was very experienced. But one day, climbing down from a roof, the ladder slipped causing him to jump from two stories above ground. He managed to land on his feet and, at first, was relieved that he had not hurt himself, or worse, hit is head. However, when he tried to put weight on his leg, it collapsed. Immediately he knew it was severe.

The ambulance transported Steve to a local hospital, but they didn't have the experience or knowledge to handle such a complicated break. Steve asked them to transfer him to a high-level trauma hospital. On arrival, the medical staff's faces told the story - the bones in his right leg had broken into small pieces. The doctor said there were too many pieces to count. Worse still was the complication of Compartmental Syndrome. This syndrome is a condition that causes the body to 'cut off' the damaged part of the body. Eight hours later, my husband had his leg cut open down both sides to relieve the pressure building up in his leg.

Fortunately, the doctor's quick response saved Steve's leg, at least for now. In the two weeks that followed, Steve underwent three additional surgeries to reconstruct his leg, with 18 screws and two plates fitted. The doctor warned me that Steve would likely be in constant pain and disabled for the rest of his life. After checking on Steve, the doctor was amazed at my husband's resilience! Steve did around-the-clock icing on his leg to control the swelling.

This isn't the end of the story. Steve's leg became infected two months later, and the doctor had to remove all the metal supporting his leg. The bones in his leg were cleaned to eliminate the infection, and the doctor warned me to prepare for his leg to be amputated. The doctor said amputation would be better than the constant pain and lack of movement. He went on to assure me there are excellent prosthetics. What a blow!

Two more surgeries followed. The doctor used cement to hold the bones together because metal couldn't be used again. Amazingly, after a month of potent antibiotics and four more months of intense therapy, the leg held together! Steve's leg healed so well that he can now walk without pain (although he can't feel much below his knee) and can even run if needed!

His doctor was confused. He said that he had never seen such a severe injury heal so well without significant consequences to functionality. The doctor admitted the healing wasn't entirely the result of his skilsl. He felt there were outside forces that helped Steve.

We had prayed, and what a miracle! God had given the doctor the skill and the knowledge to make it happen. Steve lost 15% of his bone mass below his knee, with severe infection running through his remaining bones. Not even the best doctor, his doctor, could take full credit for Steve's healing.

Proof #7: Why God Is Necessary for Rationality

There is another philosophical debate based on Rationalism which assumes the existence of God since humans have logic and morals. It is called the Transcendental Arguement put forward by Immanuel Kant in 1763. It forms the basis of modern-day Christian apologetics. 'Apologetics' is defined as defending doctrine through discussion and debate.

Transcendental reasoning is discerning how fundamental ideas of understanding are needed for us to have experiences in this world. Kant believed that human knowledge is derived from sensory involvement shaped by the mind. This is how we organize and make sense of our perceptions. Kant says transcendental reasoning assists us in closing the gap between the empirical (actual experience) and rationality or logic. He reasoned that all sensory experience must be filtered through abstract concepts or 'categories.' Donald Whitney, Professor of Biblical Spirituality, says: "*The hard consequence of Kant's theology is that nothing is knowable as it is but only as the mind perceives it.*" (From his paper titled: A Description and Analysis of the Transcendental Argument for the Existence of God)

Rationalism argues ample knowledge is known about God through unaided human understanding and rational thinking. In other words, a sensible human can think specific thoughts that cause him to come to conclusions about God.

The Ashari Islamic theologians from medieval times formed a transcendental argument that morality and logic cannot be understood except by epiphany. They also stated that belief in the Quran was necessary to interpret our world.

The Transcendental argument or Rationalism puts forward the following concepts:

1. God is a prerequisite for logic and morality.

2. Universal, immaterial, and abstract realities in people depend upon logic and morality to exist in a materialist universe.

3. We could not count on reason, morality, and logic if God didn't exist. These are required to live in the universe, which could not exist without standards or an absolute Lawgiver.

Personal Insight

The transcendental argument presents morality and logic cannot be understood except by epiphany or divine revelation.

Doing a Bible study helped me explore various points of view or arguments. I found clarity in how the different Bible chapters work together. I learned about the Old Testament and God's promises to humanity. Reading the New Testament helps me understand what Jesus did for us and how His teachings give us solutions to everyday problems. I better understand God and His desires for us after reading His word. I feel I can now apply the Bible teachings to my life.

"Do not be conformed to this world, but be transformed by the renewal of your mind, that by testing you may discern

what is the will of God, what is good and acceptable and perfect." (English Standard Version, The Bible Romans 12:2)

Reason #8: Our Sense of Right and Wrong Points to God

Where does our moral code come from? Transidatalism states God is a prerequisite to morality. One of the most well-known arguments for God's existence centers around our ability to discern right from wrong. It presumes our moral values are objective and outside of ourselves. Morality is measured by some standard of truth that exists independently of us. Does an all-powerful source, or a "Moral Lawgiver," determine this standard of truth?

From the earliest of times, men have asked these same questions. Is our natural impulse to do what's beneficial for our survival and procreation merely the result of biology and evolution, or is there something more profound, such as a perfect standard that originates from outside ourselves? Saint Augustine (A.D. 354 – 430), an early theologian and philosopher, talked about the "eternal law" or a plan where 'reason' and 'divine will' created an innate order written in the human soul.

Certain behaviors or actions have been labeled 'wrong' throughout history and globally in most cultures. For instance, murder, theft, and dishonesty are universally unacceptable. If moral codes were dependent on a human community forming them, they would differ vastly from culture to culture or, in some cases, even be non-existent. But, since moral values are consistent across many centuries, cultures, and locations, they did not originate within a human community but from an external source or lawgiver. As known by many, this source is God.

We cannot call something good or bad without basing our opinion on a standard to measure it. The standard must be objective. It can't fluctuate according to our tastes or experiences. It has to be a standard set outside of ourselves.

If there is no objective morality, there is no meaning to words such as 'good,' 'bad,' 'evil,' etc. There is no base or standard by which to judge their definition. If we attempt to convince someone of wrongdoing based on our moral convictions or standards, they are not obliged to listen since our beliefs are subjective. On the other hand, if our convictions are of an objective standard, then there is an obligation to comply.

Louie Vassalos, a theological student and financial analyst, says, "*For objective moral values to be rationally sound, they require a firm (ontological) grounding – not unlike in the construction of a structurally sound house. They stand on a foundation – one that is strong enough to bear the weight of the object that rests on it.*" (God's Existence: The Basis for Object Moral Values, 2018, March 9, TGC, Canadian Edition)

Divine Command Theory

Divine Command Theory states morality stems from God and that we have a moral obligation to obey His commands.

1. The Divine Lawgiver (God) has commanded what is moral and immoral.

2. God's commandments impose moral obligations on us.

3. Obligations arise from imperatives issued by a qualified authority. Across history and everyday life, you can see humans driven by the same inescapable laws.

4. There is a common belief in all the same imperatives that drive us.

5. God is the definition of good, and his commands and values reflect his moral character.

A final point that shows the validity of Divine Command Theory is well-stated in an article in The Internet Encyclopedia of Philosophy: "*That is, if the origin of the universe is a personal moral being, then the existence of objective moral truths are at home, so to speak, in the universe. By contrast, if the universe's origin is non-moral, then the existence of such truths becomes philosophically perplexing because it is unclear how moral properties can come into existence via non-moral origins.*"

Professor of Philosophy William Lane Craig says, "*Using the scientific method, you could never make statements about ethics, for example, about what's right and wrong, good or bad. Moral values aren't found in a test tube.*" (Reasonable Faith Podcast, Expelled: No Intelligence Allowed, 6/23/2008, 15:13)

If science can't detect or produce morality, how do humans have an inherent sense of right and wrong? Where does it come from? What or who gives humans the intelligence to know that actions have consequences and the capacity to choose to go ahead anyway or to avoid specific risky behavior?

The logical answer to these questions is you have a moral code and an inherent sense of right and wrong that is an intrinsic part of you. We are driven by an underlying belief that it is good to be honest and to love others. After all, you most likely aspire to be a good person or work with integrity because you understand these traits benefit others and satisfy yourself.

Personal Insights

Have you ever met a perfect person or been perfect yourself? Sure, you may have met people who are better, kinder, and more honest than most, but have you ever met someone who is, in every sense of the word, devoid of moral wrongdoing? We cannot be perfect, which God is well aware of. That is why He made provision for us to deal with misconduct and the resulting guilt. He sent His Son, Jesus Christ, as an atoning sacrifice to deal with our wrongdoing.

We all want to know the truth of existential questions that tug at our intellect and emotions. Itt is reasonable to assume we are not merely made up of matter but beings with a body, soul, and spirit. Our spirit profoundly believes we are here for more than this tangible world. We were each made for something or someone in which we find peace and satisfaction. This is why we need to worship. C.S. Lewis, the writer, scholar, and theologian, summed it up, *"If I find in myself desires which nothing in this world can satisfy, the only logical explanation is that I was made for another world."* (Mere Christianity by C.S Lewis)

The Bible tells us how to worship.

"Do not love the world or the things in the world. If anyone loves the world, the love of the Father is not in him. For all that is in the world—the desires of the flesh and the desires of the eyes and pride of life—is not from the Father but is from the world. And the world is passing away along with its desires, but whoever does the will of God abides forever." (English Standard Version, The Bible 1 John 2:15-17)

This chapter delved briefly into the philosophical arguments for God's existence. We explored how our innate sense of right and wrong points towards a higher power and why a creator is the explanation for the beginning of the universe. Hopefully, you've gained a deeper understanding of how truth is not a subjective concept that shifts with the passing of centuries or changes in culture.

Many of the philosophical arguments we tackled in this chapter are complex and non-empirical. They represent attributes pointing toward God, giving us a sense of order and intelligent purpose out of chaos.

CHAPTER 3

Historical Evidence for God

Scholar, author, and theologian C.S. Lewis once said, *"The greatest event in human history cannot be explained by natural causes."* What event was he referring to?

C.S. Lewis lost his mother at nine and spent much of his teen years thinking through some of life's most pressing questions. At 14, Lewis was sent to study under William Kirkpatrick, who initially influenced him to become an atheist. However, in his 30s, Lewis converted to Christianity and spent the rest of his life as a theologian looking for evidence to support his beliefs.

The event Lewis referred to is the resurrection of Jesus Christ. Many other scholars and historians have debated the validity of the Bible and searched for evidence of Jesus and his resurrection.

Reason #9: Why We Can Trust the Gospels

Skeptics have questioned whether the four gospels (the books of Matthew, Mark, Luke, and John) in the New Testament of the Bible are true. There have been accusations that the records handed down through history are untrustworthy. So, this brings us to the question: Are the accounts of Jesus in the four gospels accurate? Karlo Broussard, an apologist and speaker on biblical studies, theology, and philosophy, uses these three questions to explain how we can test the validity or reliability of the gospels.

Were the Gospel writers *able* to write reliable history?

Did the Gospel writers *intend* to write reliable history?

Did the Gospel writers *write* reliable history?

Let's see how we can answer these questions.

1. Gospel Writers Were Able to Write Reliable History

The writers of the Gospels retold eyewitness accounts. Matthew and John were disciples of Jesus and observed the events themselves, but they would have also been close friends or acquaintances with other eyewitnesses. Mark and Luke worked with and collaborated with the Apostle Paul. Mark was also a student of Peter. For historical research, eyewitness accounts are favored as evidence. Bible scholar Dr. Brant Pitre has verified that all the ancient manuscripts have the original names attributed to them.

Apart from eyewitness authorship, the timing for the Gospels lines up with them being written shortly after these events. Historians also favor eyewitness accounts written close to the event, as they are the most likely to be accurate.

This reduces the possibility that memory has faded or core details must be remembered or clarified.

Let's have a look at the timelines. Matthew and Mark would have been written around 64 - 68 A.D., 31 to 35 years after Jesus' death, while Peter and Paul were still alive. We know that their deaths were shortly after Nero persecuted the Christians. We can pinpoint the timing of Luke's writing of 'The Acts of the Apostles' to around 60 - 62 A.D. because Luke talks about Paul being under house arrest, and most historians concur with these dates. The book of Acts was written after Luke wrote the gospel of Luke. We also know that as a doctor, Luke was an upstanding member of society and would have damaged his reputation by writing fictitious accounts. The likelihood of his avoiding this risk also adds credibility to his writings.

It is important to note many eyewitnesses would have been alive when the gospels were written. This has a twofold effect on the reliability of the gospels. Firstly, the writers had many sources to draw the information and verify the facts. Secondly, it means their writings would have been criticized and refuted had they been inaccurate.

It is logical to trust the writings of men done just 30 years after events. These events were drawn from many eyewitness accounts with their reputations on the line. The writers were disciples of Jesus who traveled and lived with Him for three years, receiving daily instructions and observing his miracles. They retaught what they learned from Jesus. The disciples would have rehearsed and written his teachings down, ingraining them into their memory. These men came from Hebrew and Greek cultures, where memorizing large amounts of information was normal.

Having conceded that the writings are reliable accounts of history, let's look at the intention behind these writings.

2. Gospel Writers Intended to Write Reliable History

One of the main reasons historians believe the gospel writers intended to write reliable accounts of history is the attention to detail. This amount of detail is rarely found in fictitious accounts and legends. Actual events such as the Passover and the Festival of Tabernacles are mentioned. We also find real people verified from the region's history in which the events occur. Examples of these high-level officials are Pontius Pilate, Caiaphas the High Priest, Caesar Augustus, and Tiberius Caesar. These names and events can be verified from the first century, and we can conclude that the Gospel writers were meant to have accurate records of history.

The writers' intention to write accurate history is declared. Quoting from the writer John, we read, "*He who saw it has borne witness—his testimony is true, and he knows that he tells the truth—that you also may believe.*" (English Standard Version, The Bible John 19:35).

The writer Luke says something similar in his opening words in the Book of Acts, "*In the first book, O Theophilus,*

I have dealt with all that Jesus began to do and teach, until the day when he was taken up after he had given commands through the Holy Spirit to the apostles whom he had chosen." (English Standard Version, The Bible Acts 1:1 - 2)

Biblical scholar Dr. Pitre verifies the writings of Luke are consistent with other historical reports by Herodotus, Thucydides, and Josephus. In the original manuscript, Luke uses the word *diēgēsis*, Greek for "narrative." Greco-Roman authors used this word specifically for writing historical accounts. Luke draws attention to the fact that he uses eyewitness reports, making it possible for readers to verify his writing. Luke tells us his purpose is to declare the truth about what happened. His words further expose him to criticism if his account of the events is incorrect. Later in the chapter, he uses another Greek word, *asphaleia*, which means "the facts." Therefore, it is reasonable to accept that Luke intended to write an accurate historical account of the events.

Matthew and Luke include the family tree of Jesus, further reinforcing the historical aspect. This was typical of history's writing style, particularly biographies from that era.

Historians concur the writers from that time wrote more in themes or according to a topic as they remembered the events and were not too concerned about chronological order. We read at the end of the Gospel of John, *"Now there are also many other things which Jesus did; were every one of them to be written, I suppose that the world itself*

could not contain the books that would be written."
(English Standard Version, The Bible John 21:25)

This style is similar to the writings of Plutarch, the Greek historian, in his biography of Alexander the Great and Lucian when he wrote the *Life of Demonax.*

3. Gospel Writers Did Write Reliable History

We can verify the validity of the historical context of the Gospels through the criteria that historians use to verify a saying or event. The most popular standard is *multiple attestation* or the occurrence of the writing from more than one source. The Gospels, written by four different writers, the letters written by the Apostle Paul, reports by early church clergy, first-century Jewish historians, and the first-century Roman historian Tacitus, are consistent with the gospels' details.

Other criteria for verifying accuracy are:

- *Embarrassment* or the inclusion of details that possibly appear to negate the original purpose without the writer needing to defend his position and

- *Coherence* or the correlation of details tying up with known historical events.

The accounts of Jesus' death particularly fit these criteria. There is also archaeological evidence to back up the writings of the Gospels.

Here are a few examples, although there are many more:

- In the 19th century, the pool of Bethesda mentioned in John 5 was discovered.

- An inscription with Pontius Pilate's name was discovered in Caesarea in 1961.

- The same year, a Maritima of a third-century mosaic in Caesarea was discovered with the name "Nazareth" in it.

- Coins have been unearthed with the names of Herod the King, Herod the Tetrarch of Galilee, Herod Agrippa I, and Herod Agrippa II, all mentioned in the Gospels for, respectively, beheading John the Baptist, killing James Zebedee, and presiding over the trial of Paul the Apostle.

- 1990, a container with the inscribed Aramaic words "Joseph son of Caiaphas" was discovered.

- A vault was discovered in 1968 with the bones of a first-century man, confirming the details of a crucifixion-type death similar to the description of the death of Jesus.

- An inscription dated between 14 - 37 B.C. records the temple dedication and mentions Lysanius Tetrarch of Abila, referred to by Luke in Luke 3:1.

Non-biblical writers from the first century, such as the historian Josephus, have details in their writings that verify those given in the Gospels. The High Priests Caiaphas, Annas, Pontius Pilate, and King Herod are mentioned. There are accounts of John the Baptist being beheaded by King Herod, mention of Jesus as a 'wise man' and 'doer of startling deeds,' and being sentenced to death by 'Pontius Pilate.'

Cornelius Tacitus, a first-century historian, talks about a group of people called "Christians" In his work *The Annals.* He describes their leader as 'Christus,' who was "put to death by Pontius Pilate, procurator of Judea during the time of Tiberius." (*Annals* 15.44)

Since the account of events given to us by the Gospel writers are backed by other historical writings and archeological findings, and collaborate with ancient non-Christian sources, we can reasonably believe the writers, Matthew, Mark, Luke, and John, gave us reliable accounts of actual history. We also find the writers themselves made claims about where they got their inspiration for writing. When writing to Timothy, Paul stated, "*All Scripture is breathed out by God and profitable for teaching, for reproof, for correction, and for training in righteousness, [...]*" (English Standard Version, The Bible 2 Timothy 3:16)

Peter wrote many letters to the early Christians, stating, "*[...] knowing this first of all, that no prophecy of Scripture comes from someone's own interpretation. For no prophecy was ever produced by the will of man, but men spoke from God as they were carried along by the Holy Spirit. "*(English Standard Version, The Bible 2 Peter 1: 20 - 21)

Trustworthiness of the Gospels

Usually, if a storyteller tries to convince someone that a made-up story is true, they add copious amounts of detail. Only the essential facts are included when recording history, and the assumption is that those reading the account will already be familiar with some of the details. There is no need to go overboard, convincing the reader. We find this style to be true in the writings of the Gospels. Some pieces are omitted on the assumption that the reader will already have the information.

Here is an example: From other historical writings, we know that some of the controversies in the early church threatened to split the group. Luke referred to this debate as' no small dissension' in Acts 15:2. But instead of inventing teachings attributed to Jesus, the writers remain faithful to His message, reiterating that Jesus taught that to have eternal life, it was necessary to believe in Jesus. They kept the teachings of Jesus pure, accurate, and undiluted without reinforcing the issue. When the writer does not portray his opinion, the writer will likely record events accurately.

The Apostle Paul also keeps his writing accurate and responsibly stated when expressing his opinion. Some of

Paul's letters were written before the Gospels. There would be the temptation to use his influentience as a leader to take his opinions and instructions and attribute them to Jesus. However, we do not see that in the Gospels. Jesus did not give teachings on many issues the early church had to deal with. He could not since He had already ascended to Heaven. Jesus did promise the gift of the Holy Spirit to guide and lead, and that is from whom the Apostle Paul gained his wisdom.

The Date of the New Testament Writings

Three of the four Gospel writers recorded Jesus' prophecy that the temple in Jerusalem would be destroyed, yet none recorded the actual event. Since this only occurred in 70 A.D., they were no longer around to do so. Thus, we can conclude that the Gospels were written before this.

Luke is considered the most highly educated and accurate of the writers. He accurately refers to 32 countries, 54 cities, and nine islands. Modern-day maritime maps have verified the details of Paul's journey from Palestine to Italy.

According to one of the most respected Biblical New Testament scholars, FF Bruce, the writings of Luke are accurate. He says, *"A man whose accuracy can be demonstrated in matters where we are able to test it is likely to be accurate even where the means for testing him are not available. Accuracy is a habit of mind, and we know from happy experiences that some people are habitually accurate just as others can be depended upon to be inaccurate. Luke's record entitles him to be regarded as a writer of habitual accuracy."*

The book of Acts features the Temple in Jerusalem as playing a central role in the life of the early Christians. From this we can deduce that the book was written before the temple was destroyed in 70 A.D. At the end of the book, Luke describes Paul's house arrest but does not mention his death nor the death of Peter, although he describes the deaths of both Stephen and James. This helps us to date the book before 64 A.D. Since he records the deaths of two prominent people in the group he would have recorded the deaths of two leaders, unless they had not happened at the time of writing. In Paul's letter to Timothy, he quotes from Luke's writing, indicating that the Gospel of Luke was indeed completed during Paul's lifetime.

Verifying the dates of these writings is vital because it helps prove the accounts' accuracy. The historian A.N. Sherwin White has done an in-depth analysis showing that it takes two generations of retelling events before myths and inaccuracies develop since eyewitnesses will correct these inaccuracies before they pass them on. Several original manuscripts, the Bibical Paprus, including the Chester Beatty Papyri from 250 A.D., contain most New Testament writings from the Book of John. The Bodmer Papyri, dated 200 A.D., also includes most of the book of John. Another manuscript, the Rylands Papyri, found in Egypt and dated

120 A.D., also has most of the Book of John. It is widely held that these manuscripts were John's hand-copied writings so they could be dispersed. These manuscripts all help to verify the Gospels were written within the lifespan of the eyewitnesses who would correct any inaccuracies.

Archaeology and the Gospels

Earlier in this chapter, we examined a few archaeological examples. Still, according to Randall Price, an archaeologist, more than 100,000 archaeological pieces of evidence prove biblical references.

Evidence that Pontius Pilate, who is prominently featured in all accounts of Jesus' trial and crucifixion, existed can be verified by the discovery in 1961 by Antonio Frova, an Italian archaeologist. A fragment of a plaque from the steps leading up to the Caesarea Theater has the inscription, *"Pontius Pilatus, Prefect of Judea, has dedicated to the people of Caesarea a temple in honor of Tiberius."* (Original in Latin) Chronologically, this fits with the New Testament that records Pontius Pilot as Curator between 26 - 36 A.D.

Non-biblical Corroboration of the Gospels

In his statement, a first-century Roman historian named Tacitus confirms that Pilate was a procurator. *"Christus, from whom the name had its origin, suffered the extreme penalty during the reign of Tiberius at the hands of one of our procurators, Pontius Pilatus. . . ."* ("Being Called "Kirisuto-san" or "a Christ\U27": Re-visiting Christian Identity in Post-disaster Japan." 2016, https://core.ac.uk/download/230284650.pdf.)

Thallus, a writer of Greek history, is quoted by Julius Africanus in 221 A.D. He collaborates with the Gospel account that darkness covered the Earth when Jesus died, attributed to a solar eclipse. His writings show that the story of Jesus' crucifixion was well-known in Rome.

The *Talmud,* by Jewish writers and completed in 300 A.D, talks about Jesus as a significant figure but labels Him as a heretic. This fact is not surprising since Jesus challenged the teachings of the Jewish leaders and scholars while He lived.

The writings of Josephus, another first-century historian, also talk about the Kings named Herod and the Emperors Augustus, Tiberius, Claudius, and Nero. His reports mention the High Priests Caiaphas, Ananias, and Annas, further corroborating the validity of the Gospels.

The deaths of Agrippa, John the Baptist, and the death of James are all documented. These writings verify the characters and events we read about in the Gospels.

The Manuscript Evidence

Since we have evidence of corroboration between the Gospels and non-biblical writings, we must also check whether these manuscripts are accurate.

There are 24,000 documents from which we can draw the information:

- 5,000 Greek manuscripts from the first century
- Quotes from early church leaders
- Translations such as the Latin Vulgate

Some of these early church fathers, such as Clement of Rome (95 A.D.), Polycarp (110-150 A.D.), and The Shepherd of Hermas, quote from the gospels and Paul's letters or refer to these writings. With the time gap of twenty-five years between the oldest New Testament manuscripts and original papers, we can be confident we have an accurate account. With so many manuscripts, it is easy to compare to ensure accuracy. The New Testament scholar Bruce Metzger says we have a New Testament that is 99.5% accurate to the original text.

So, What Was the Impact That Jesus Had on the World?

No other living person has ever had the same impact as Jesus. He is the most talked about, debated, referred to, and disputed person to have ever lived. He has also had the most significant positive impact on those who have engaged and encountered Him—more than any other world leader or influencer.

His initial followers were devastated at his death but irrevocably changed when they met Him after His resurrection. Initial skeptics were now willing to be persecuted, tortured, and killed as martyrs after His resurrection. The Apostle Paul, originally known as Saul of Tarsus, was one of the most prominent critics, persecuting the early Christians vehemently until his encounter on the road to Damascus. We have to take note of the change that took place in him because afterwards the early church embraced Paul. He became the most avid leader among them, traveling tirelessly to spread the Gospel of Jesus Christ.

Perhaps the influence of Jesus can be summed up by quoting the historian Philip Schaff: *"This Jesus of Nazareth, without money and arms, conquered more millions than Alexander, Caesar, Mohammed, and Napoleon; without science [...] he shed more light on things human and divine than all philosophers and scholars combined; without the eloquence of schools, he spoke such words of life as were never spoken before or since, and produced effects which lie beyond the reach of orator or poet; without writing a single line, he set more pens in motion, and furnished themes for more sermons, orations, discussions, learned volumes, works of art, and songs of praise than the whole army of great men of ancient and modern times."* (Influence - North Florida Fellowship of Christian Peace Officers. https://northfloridafcpo.org/devotion/influence/)

Jesus taught the people to love, saying this would be the most distinguishing characteristic of His followers. He encouraged a love for God and love for those in the immediate family, community, and broader society.

Following on from love was His message of forgiveness. Jesus preached God's forgiveness through the laying down of His own life, but also taught His followers to forgive those who wronged them. Jesus taught His followers to be responsible citizens by encouraging them to pay taxes and help others.

Provision through trusting God was demonstrated when Jesus prayed over two fish and five loaves of bread then told His disciples to feed the crowd. There was more than enough for everyone to eat. The scraps picked up afterward filled 12 baskets. Although this event demonstrated God's ability to provide miraculously, it was also a lesson in compassion and assistance for his followers. Jesus saw that the crowd was hungry, had empathy for them, and did something about their plight by feeding them.

Jesus often challenged the religious leaders of His culture, particularly in showing kindness and speaking to women who were use to being shunned and rejected. We read examples where He healed a woman who was not to be out publicly according to their laws. Jesus spoke to the prostitute at the well, forgiving her and changing the direction of her life. He assisted a woman who was about to be stoned by the crowd. Jesus looked at their needs and ignored what the community thought about them.

There were many other teachings, and in his Epistles, Plinius Secundus, a Roman Governor, wrote that the early Christians loved others. He was often confounded and affected by their love when he ordered them to be executed for refusing to deny Jesus. Plinius said, *"[...] their firm commitment not to do any wicked deeds, never to commit any fraud, theft, adultery, never to falsify their word, not to deny a trust when they should be called upon to deliver it up."*

Personal Insights

Jesus challenged the popular trends, opinions, and culture of His society. He showed us why it is vital to consider what we accept and ensure it aligns with our convictions. We need to be critical of what we believe is the truth.

For centuries, many have started as agnostics, atheists, non-believers, or simply indifferent but have later become some of the most prominent voices claiming that Jesus Christ is the Son of God, our hope for salvation.

The Bible tells us:

"Because, if you confess with your mouth that Jesus is Lord and believe in your heart that God raised him from the dead, you will be saved." (English Standard Version, The Bible Romans 10:9)

Reason #10: The Truth of the Resurrection

Throughout history, from the beginnings of the early church, it is written that although Jesus died, He also rose again. Jesus' resurrection sets Christianity apart from all other religions - a *living* God is the object of worship. So, is there any actual evidence to substantiate this claim?

One of the most defining pieces of evidence is that the location of Jesus's burial is well known and can be visited today, empty. The resurrection of Christ is a pivotal point. Without a living Christ, there is no point in Christianity. The Apostle Paul made it clear when he wrote to the church at Corinth: *"If Christ has not been raised, your faith is futile; you are still in your sins... [and] we are to be pitied more than all men."* (English Standard Version, The Bible 1 Corinthians 15:17-19)

We are talking about a physical return to life, not vague imagery. It's also important to note that Paul makes this point clear when writing to the Corinthians, who were influenced by the Greek philosophies of Platonism (existence of abstract objects) and Dualism (opposites can be true simultaneously).

The Resurrection of Jesus is the most disputed aspect of Christianity with many conspiracy theories, so it is essential to look at each. We will then reconsider and examine the proof that exists.

Conspiracy Hypothesis

The early disciples were aware of the rumors circulating that one of them had stolen the body of Jesus to stage his resurrection. We can read about this in Matthew 28:11. Modern biblical scholars believe it would have been complicated to get so many people to produce such a hoax. They would risk their lives holding to the lie due to their deep belief in the resurrection. The scholars also believe such a hoax would not have entered the disciples' minds. The disciples believed Jesus was the Messiah, and their despair at His death would have immobilized them from taking further action.

Apparent Death Theory

The claim is that Jesus was not wholly dead when his body was removed from the cross and He escaped the tomb after three days of rest. This claim can easily be refuted: His injuries after being severely beaten and nailed to a cross, including having his side and lungs pierced by a sword, were so severe that it is not medically possible for Him to have recovered in that short space of time. The leading cause of death in crucifixion is suffocation due to the body's position, causing the lungs to collapse. Could He have recovered sufficiently after three days to remove a heavy stone, which took several people to roll into place? And, could He have overpowered armed Roman guards?

The Roman soldiers, experts in execution and dealing with a man they believed to have committed treason, would have thoroughly checked that Jesus was dead. Because Jesus had prophesied that He would rise from the dead after three days, orders were given to seal the stone and guard the tomb. This fact alone would have made it impossible for Jesus to escape the tomb.

Wrong Tomb Theory

This theory claims the women who went to the tomb were at the wrong place and frightened by a caretaker's statement that Jesus was not there. The claim is dispelled by biblical scholars who point out that Jesus appeared to many people after His resurrection. A conspiracy theory of this magnitude would have been almost impossible to orchestrate by the disciples. The tomb belonged to a prominent person, Joseph of Arimathea, so it is unlikely that the women were confused about the location.

Displaced Body Theory

Another theory claims Joseph of Arimathea moved the body from his tomb, giving the disciples cause to claim Jesus had risen. Once again, this discounts the many appearances of Jesus after His resurrection. Also, it dismisses the sealing of the tomb with the stone and the armed guards. Too many people were aware of the tomb where Jesus was laid. With accusations against him, Joseph would have shown where the new grave was, clearing his name.

Post-resurrection Appearances of Jesus

There are several pieces of evidence for the appearance of Jesus after his resurrection.

Jesus prophesied his Resurrection: Jesus was very open with his disciples about what would happen to Him. He talked about the opposition by elders, chief priests, and law teachers. Jesus told the disciples He would be killed and raised to life on the third day.

The only explanation for an empty tomb: There is no other proven reason for the empty tomb, and we have established it would have been impossible for Jesus to escape. Also, Jesus had been tightly wrapped in burial cloths, making it difficult to move with such extensive injuries. Discarding the grave clothes would have presented a problem. At the very least, they would have been bloody. Jesus would have appeared in public without appropriate clothes or bloody clothes. Jesus would of been easily spotted. He still had the scars on His hands where the nails had been.

He appeared to many people: If you want to fabricate a conspiracy, keep it to as few people as possible so the real truth can't leak. Yet, Jesus was seen by many people, some of whom were not his disciples. He appeared to two travelers on the road to Emmaus.

Resurrection is the reason for the beginning of Christianity: Jesus demonstrated His ability to overcome death. The disciples and the sisters of Lazarus witnessed Jesus raising Lazarus from the dead after four days.

When Jesus died, his disciples were filled with despair. Men in this state cannot start one of the most significant movements ever and sustain it as the disciples did.

Change in the disciples: Something phenomenal changed these men between the time Jesus was taken from the cross and His resurrection. Initially, they were afraid and went into hiding, cowering immediately after Jesus' death. After His resurrection, Jesus told the disciples He had to go away (ascend to Heaven) for the Holy Spirit to come. The disciples became completely different people. They immediately went out to spread the news, forming the first church. The disciples became bold and assertive in their faith.

The change in critics: Many were critical of the new Christians. Remember Saul, who we mentioned earlier? In the Bible, we read how Saul persecuted Christians, ordering their deaths. But when Saul encountered Jesus while on his way to Damascus, Saul was utterly transformed. Saul's change of heart and soul was so extreme he was accepted into the church. Eventually, Saul became an Apostle and leader. The difference can only be explained by his encounter with the resurrected Christ. Read more about Saul, who became Paul, in Acts 9:1-20.

The Existence of Christianity

In the Old Testament, the coming of the Messiah was someone victorious who would rule, not a victim of crucifixion and death. The resurrection reversed the calamity of Jesus's death. His identity as the Messiah was fulfilled as it had been proclaimed.

Throughout history, the birth, death, and resurrection of Jesus Christ has globally celebrated. His birth is the framework for our calendar. Scholars of the Old Testament prophecies regarding a Messiah have matched over 100 texts to these widely accepted historical events. Regardless of your opinion, the fact is there are millions of people around the world and throughout past centuries who believe in Jesus Christ and the validity of the Bible.

According to The Pew Research Center, an American think tank based in Washington, D.C., Christianity is still the world's largest religion. The center provides information on social issues, public opinion, and demographic trends shaping the United States and the world. The largest religion in 2020 was Christianity, at 31.1%.

Personal Insights

One of my friends most defining moments in his faith journey was traveling to Israel to see many places mentioned in the Bible where Jesus walked. The historical sights mentioned in the Bible can be visited in person. Standing on the Mount of Olives, looking toward the

Eastern wall of Jerusalem, gave him a sense of the scene described in Luke 19, where Jesus descended the mountain and went into Jerusalem.

He observed the mountainside referred to in the account of the crucifixion called the 'place of the skull.' The rock face looks like a skull with two cavities where the eyes would have been and a hole almost centered where the mouth would have been. But the most awe-inspiring moment was when he stood in the garden looking into the empty tomb of Jesus.

"For I delivered to you as of first importance what I also received: that Christ died for our sins in accordance with the Scriptures, that he was buried, that he was raised on the third day in accordance with the Scriptures, and that he appeared to Cephas, then to the twelve. Then he appeared to more than five hundred brothers at one time, most of whom are still alive, though some have fallen asleep. Then he appeared to James, then to all the apostles. ..." (English Standard Version, The Bible 1 Corinthians 15:3-8)

I hope some of your questions have been answered, but we are not finished. There are still many more questions to be answered.

CHAPTER 4

Objections and Difficult Questions

We have established that the four Gospels, the primary source of the life of Jesus, can be trusted as accurate. We've shown that the core of Christianity is based is the resurrection of Jesus and a living God seting it apart from all other religions. Now, we will look at some of the questions most of us grapple with.

One of the most asked questions relates to the seeming contradiction of God's loving nature and the apparent evil in our universe causing suffering. We'll also look at the basis for God giving us 'free will,' God's nature as a triune God, the existence of hell, and religious diversity.

Reason #11: Why God Allows Suffering

Generally, suffering in our world can be defined as bad or "evil" by most accounts. Our dilemma with evil stems from our concept of God. We believe God is perfect (omnibenevolent), absolutely powerful (omnipotent), and knowledgeable about all things (omniscient). So, we become confused about how a God with these characteristics could create a world containing evil. If God is all knowledgeable, He must know about evil before it happens. And, if God is all-powerful, He could stop evil. So why does He not stop it? Surely, if He is all good, He would want to stop the evil. We can't understand why He does nothing about it.

These are questions that have puzzled many, including theologians and philosophers. Let's see if our concept of God is correct or if there are other factors at work that allow evil.

We are looking at 'evil' in a broader sense, not just that which we can assign to the actions of humans or supernatural forces. There are two general categories of evil on Earth:

1. Moral evil

Here we are talking about defiant actions humans commit, such as theft, murder, rape, arson, etc. There is always an initiator or wrongdoer committing an intentional or negligent act and a victim/s suffering pain or loss.

2. Natural evil

By 'natural evil,' we mean hardship created by famine, floods, earthquakes, etc. Natural evil can be separated into 'physical evil' or that which causes bodily and mental pain, and 'metaphysical evil,' which is brought about by chance imperfections such as deformities or injustice when criminals are not punished.

To a certain extent, we can rationalize natural evil through the scientific processes we observe, giving a degree of acceptance. However, having moral evil in our world causes us to doubt God's existence. Our concept of Him is contrary to what we sometimes experience. We may argue if God exists, there would be no hardships or natural evil. But, there is evil, so therefore, we conclude that God does not exist.

The Logical Problem of Evil

Our problem relates to what appears to be a contradiction in our idea of God. We perceive Him as a perfect being that is all good and all-powerful yet allows evil. One way to resolve this seeming disagreement in our perception of God and corruption is to hold humans responsible. However, more is needed to solve the issue. We would say that although God can, He does not stop evil and created the agents that cause sin. Saying God knows beforehand of the evil and capacity to generate it but does not stop it questions whether He is all-knowing and all-powerful.

There are four responses to this train of thought:

- 'Theodicy' holds that our idea of God as all good and all-powerful can co-exist with the presence of evil.
- 'Transformation of Evil' states there is no evil.
- 'Process Theology' changes the idea of God to something other than all-good and all-powerful.

- Atheism holds that there is no God, so there is no problem with evil and its relationship to God.

It appears our concept of God needs adjusting. So, where does our idea of God come from?

Our beliefs in our world are shaped by hearing accounts, stories, and what we observe. This is how we develop assumptions and our general thought processes. At first, we mold our thinking so that our immediate group accepts us, and we spend little time reflecting on our beliefs. Critical thinking is unnecessary if the rest of our group thinks the same way. Any new thoughts are evaluated in the current context, and if they are consistent with what we already believe, then we accept them as accurate. This is called the 'coherentist theory of truth.'

Eventually, we learn to reflect and be critical of thought processes, and inconsistencies may appear. As we come into contact with a broader group, our concepts and beliefs are expanded and sometimes accepted too hastily. New information can cause contradictions with our core beliefs, which are not abandoned, but we find ways to bring in qualifiers and alternate interpretations to preserve our belief system. We continue to bring in further qualifiers that burden our fundamental beliefs, which then come under scrutiny, and the need for a new alternate belief system arises.

This observation goes back to the time of Socrates, Plato, and Aristotle, who saw inconsistencies in the Greek deities. Our perceptions of God are the problem. God describes Himself as loving and holy but also absolutely just. He will act in our best interest, which may contradict our desires. God cannot do evil or sin. He is fair and just, meaning that wrongdoing must be punished. God can use whatever He deems to persuade people to turn from their morally evil ways.

"So listen to me, people of Judah and Jerusalem! I have decided to strike you with disaster, and I won't change my mind unless you stop sinning and start living right." (Contemporary English Version, the Bible Jeremiah 18:11)

The Purpose of Suffering

There is the belief that suffering comes about due to the free will that God gave to us. This theory dates back to preliterate times before we had scientific evidence that geological and physical functions cause natural disasters such as floods and earthquakes. These processes are beyond the control of human free will and affect all communities without regard for babies or animals who cannot exercise free will. Throughout history, we have seen these events happen. Natural disasters have nothing to do with people's behavior.

Physical and mental pain is real. Suffering is a part of life, so we want to understand it. We all experience some or most of the following: disappointment, loneliness, hurt, anxiety, discrimination, rejection, persecution, calamity, and trauma in varying ways.

God will use our suffering for good, whether it is natural or our own doing. There are times when God will use suffering as a form of justice.

Sometimes, suffering is a direct consequence of the choices we make. Here is a simple example. If you were to climb a tree to about 20 feet, you'd be reasonably safe on the main trunk if you held on tightly. But if you then decide to venture out towards the end of one of the thin branches at the top, it is likely to break. You will fall to the ground, possibly breaking a leg, arm, or shoulder. Is it the tree's fault that you are now suffering? Or is it simply the natural consequence of defying common sense and testing the law of gravity? Who is to blame for your suffering?

There are specific laws, values, and morals, most of which were commanded by God. If you defy these, you could suffer. So, suffering may result from our sins. A reminder that God wants the best for us, and that's why we need to obey His rules.

Suffering can be a reminder to behave responsibly and repent from our wrongdoings. It is also a reminder of what Jesus went through to atone for our sins and provide forgiveness, opening a way to God on our behalf. We are all given our cross to bear.

God is concerned with our character and holiness rather than our comfort. Helen Keller, blind author, advocate for disability rights, political activist, and lecturer, summed it up: "*Character cannot be developed in ease and quiet. Only through experience of trial and suffering can the soul be strengthened, ambition inspired, and success achieved*". (Blasingame, Thomas A. "Survive, Revive, Thrive: Chapter 11—Flank Speed." Journal of Petroleum Technology, 2021, https://doi.org/10.2118/0821-0006-jpt)

Sometimes, God allows us to suffer to learn, grow and develop. It's necessary to subject a plant to the pain of being cut back so new growth can happen. It's a similar process for us - suffering causes us to reassess, which can bring about new beginnings. The heading to this section uses the word 'sanctification,' which means 'to become holy; to purify or become free from sin.'

The Bible tells us to be like God: "*Always live as God's holy people should, because God is the one who chose you, and he is holy .*" (Contemporary English Version, The Bible 1 Peter 1:15)

God sometimes uses suffering to help us draw nearer to Him. He does not expect us to suffer alone in silence but invites us to come to Him for help. He encourages us to approach: "*So whenever we are in need, we should come bravely before the throne of our merciful God. There we will be treated with undeserved kindness, and we will find help.*" (Contemporary English Version, The Bible Hebrews 4:16)

Going through difficulty beyond our ability to fix it means we must turn to God for help and trust Him. The early Christians had this experience, "*For we do not want you to be unaware, brothers, of the affliction we experienced in Asia. For we were so utterly burdened beyond our strength that we despaired of life itself. Indeed, we felt that we had received the sentence of death. But that made us rely not on ourselves but God who raises the dead.*" (English Standard Version, The Bible 2 Corinthians 1:8 – 9)

When they did not know what to do, they called on God for help. If you are in a situation and don't know what to do, pray and ask God. He promises to give wisdom. *"If any of you lacks wisdom, let him ask God, who gives generously to all without reproach, and it will be given him."* (English Standard Version, The Bible James 1:5)

Personal insights

Suffering isn't usually from God. However, God will use our suffering for His will.

My mom unexpectedly died in 2021. The whole family was devastated. I was very close with my mom and didn't know how I would go on without her. On top of that, I am my parents' Medical Power of Attorney (POA). My dad has been ill for a few years with varying degrees of dementia, prostate cancer, heart disease, and decreased mobility. I suddenly became the decision-maker for my dad's care.

We all did the best we could. At first, my sisters and I were planning our mom's funeral and taking shifts caring for our dad. The heartache was overwhelming. We didn't have time to process. We began to argue amongst ourselves.

The result was just as devastating. For months, I felt I had lost everything. Now, I lost my mom and sisters as well. You see, during COVID, my husband and I decided to move and get a fresh start. As we moved into our new home, my husband lost his job. He was out of work for five months. I worked part-time, so I searched for a full-time job to help my family. Not only did we leave our community of 22 years, but we left all our colleagues and friends from work. We felt isolated and alone.

For me, my world had fallen apart. I had to give up my everyday life to be with my dad for about six months. My life revolved around crying and doing things for him. I finally gave up. I turned to God and pleaded for help. I was a believer but hadn't stayed connected with my spiritual life. Church services weren't live before my mom's death, and I had let my prayer time go. God used my suffering at this time to bring me back to Him.

Afterward, I found peace in my heart. I was able to reconcile with one of my sisters. My other sister and I have decided not to discuss the past and move on. We moved our dad into a great facility, so my time has been freed up to do things like writing this book. I am closer to God now than I have been in a long time, all thanks to my pled for help, returning me to a relationship with God.

Reason #12: Why Evil Is Not God's Fault

Our concept of a perfect God is challenged by the fact there is evil in the world. Many have asked why a good and loving God allows evil.

The philosopher J. L. Mackie raised the same question. Analytic philosopher Alvin Plantinga responded with what he called the 'free will defense.' He pointed out that God has put specific laws and parameters in place and will not override them to satisfy our demands. God doesn't act contrary to His nature. He has created man with free will. God will not override our free will to ensure we don't choose evil. We are free to choose either good or evil. Overriding our choice would take away our free will.

Plantinga points out it is impossible to give a creature free will and stop it from exercising said free will when it chooses to use it for evil. Doing that would take away free will and infringe on the free will principle.

The philosopher St. Augustine believed evil could be attributed to Satan and his followers. The Bible tells us that Satan was initially in Heaven with God but rebelled and was cast out with a third of the angels. Satan has been causing havoc ever since. The evil we experience is greatly influenced by the actions of Satan and his dominions.

Personal Insights

God encourages all to choose what is right. There are many verses in the Bible where we see His desires for our lives.

"My friends, you were chosen to be free. So don't use your freedom as an excuse to do anything you want. Use it as an opportunity to serve each other with love." (Contemporary English Version, The Bible Galatians 5:13)

God does not ignore the evil that happens. We read in the Bible how God promises judgment and punishment on those who continually choose to do evil without repenting and turning from their evil ways.

"For sin's meager wages is death, but God's lavish gift is life eternal, found in your union with our Lord Jesus, the Anointed One." (The Passion Translation, The Bible Romans 6:23)

God preserves our free will by offering forgiveness and salvation to those who repent. Jesus himself explained this when He said: *"I have not come to call the 'righteous,' but to call those who fail to measure up and bring them to repentance."* (The Passion Translation, The Bible Luke 5:32)

Reason #13: The Existence of Hell is Necessary and Just

Christian doctrine describes hell as one of two places available after death. Those who have faith in Jesus will be with Him in Heaven. Those who reject Jesus and refuse to repent from their wrongdoing go to hell. This distinction seems inconsistent with the concept that God is a loving Father. The Theologian C.S. Lewis wrote about hell, *"There is no doctrine which I would more willingly remove from Christianity than this if it lay in my power."* Many Christians whose family and friends have not put their faith in Jesus Christ would agree. None of us want to go to hell nor see those we love go to a place of eternal torment.

God is a Holy Being. He has given us a set of morals and standards, set out in Exodus as the Commandments. In Exodus 33:17 - 20, we read about a conversation between Moses and God. Moses asks God to physically show Himself because Moses wants to see God's glory. God responds by saying no one can see His face and still live. God did reveal Himself to Moses but told him to hide in the crevice of a rock. God covered His eyes, so all Moses saw was the back of God. It's not that Moses was too sinful (God said He was pleased with Moses). God is perfect and holy. Because God is so sacred, even the slightest sin in His presence requires death.

Truths About Hell

- *Hell is what hell is because God is who God is*

Hell is there to demonstrate the righteousness, holiness, perfection, and justice of God. If we get rid of hell, how would those who commit heinous crimes against fellow humans and refuse to repent or turn from their evil ways be punished? How would there be justice for the victims of such crimes? Hell is the result of turning away from God.

- *Jesus spoke about hell more than anyone else in Scripture*

Jesus shows tremendous love and compassion, especially for the outcasts and downtrodden. However, He was very clear about the subject of hell. Jesus encouraged his followers not to be afraid of people. Although they could hurt you physically, they could not harm your soul. He said instead to fear God, who could destroy both body and soul in hell. Jesus said that those who please God would have eternal life, but those who failed to do what God wanted would be punished forever in an everlasting fire prepared for the devil and his angels. Jesus demonstrated the high standards of God when He said, *"But I say to you that everyone angry with his brother will be liable to judgment; whoever insults his brother will be liable to the council; and whoever says, 'You fool!' will be liable to the hell of fire."* (English Standard Version, The Bible Matthew 5:22). Jesus further described hell as a place where there would be weeping and gnashing of teeth.

Having set impossible standards by His own holy and perfect nature as a measure, God also grasped our frailty as humans. God knew that we would battle to live up to any resemblance of His perfection. So, He made provision for repentance and atonement. In the Old Testament, we read how the people went once per year to offer a perfect lamb as a sacrifice for their sins to receive forgiveness—an ongoing and tedious process. In the New Testament, we learn of God's plan to offer one sacrifice for all sins, past, present, and future, to deal with this problem for all time. But there was only one candidate perfect enough to suffice - His own Son Jesus. We can read in the Gospels the graphic description of what Jesus went through to initiate our salvation and provide a way for us to gain eternal life. There are many Bible verses, but these describe it well.

"He is the propitiation for our sins, and not for ours only but also for the sins of the whole world." (English Standard Version, The Bible, 1 John 2:2)

Propitiation means to divert God's anger by offering a sacrifice, while to atone means to repay. These definitions help us to understand what Jesus did on our behalf, initiated by God Himself because of His love.

"In this is love, not that we have loved God but that he loved us and sent his Son to be the propitiation for our sins." (English Standard Version, The Bible, 1 John 4:10)

Jesus spoke about hell to warn about the danger of not accepting God's incredible gift of salvation.

God Doesn't Send Anyone to Hell; We Send Ourselves

In our limited understanding of God's ways, we feel that hell contradicts who God is, but the Bible teaches the opposite. God prefers reconciliation and forgiveness and, therefore, made a way for us by offering the most precious thing He had: His Son. We can accept God's offer of reconciliation and forgiveness and obtain eternal life or reject it and suffer the consequences of hell. C.S. Lewis, the theologian, put it like this: *"In the long run, the answer to all those who object to the doctrine of hell is itself a question: "What are you asking God to do?". . . To leave them alone? Alas, I am afraid that is what he does. . . In the end, there are only two kinds of people—those who say to God, "Thy will be done," and those to whom God says in the end, "Thy will be done."*

Who are we as creatures to question the Creator? There is a lovely analogy in the Bible about a potter forming a pot of clay the way he wants to. The clay never asks, "What are you doing? Not like that, make me like this…"

We cannot be fair and just like God is. Let's be honest: if we were to judge, those we favor would get off lightly for the worst crimes, and those we dislike would be harshly punished for minor offenses. When the Bible compares God and a human, God is the more merciful of the two.

It's tempting to think that God uses hell to coerce humans into catering to His will. It seems manipulative. But God offers salvation as an opportunity to remove the barrier (of sin) between us and God, which is the beginning of a relationship with Him. Nothing will change if you only accept Jesus to escape hell, and your heart won't be in the relationship. If you have ever experienced a relationship where one partner was not committed, you'll know how unsatisfying and problematic such a relationship is. The only way to enjoy God and Heaven is to be willingly involved.

How can a loving God send people to hell?

This is an excellent question! We tend to view God as a non-confrontational being. We expect him to be tolerant like a kind grandfather would be. However, the biblical definition of 'loving God' differs from our perception of Him. The Bible does say that God is love. Therefore, He defines love and cannot do anything unloving. So, if God is loving, then everything He does is motivated by love.

To help relate, imagine a grandpa looking after a toddler who wants to put his chubby little finger into the electrical wall socket. Grandpa has repeatedly said, "No, don't put your finger in the socket; it is dangerous." But the toddler won't listen. So, the next time the toddler tries to put his finger in the socket, Grandpa smacks his hand just hard enough to sting a little, getting his message across. Is the grandfather unfair, or is he ensuring the toddler remains safe? When God makes 'rules' for us to observe, He does it for our best interest. Is God then unfair when He punishes us for not following His ways?

Let's rephrase the question: "If God is love, then why do some people go to hell?"

Remember our earlier discussion on how we've been given free will? We have a choice to observe His law or to ignore them and suffer the consequences. The word 'send' indicates God is the only person in this scenario with a choice. That is a fallacy; we also have a choice. God has given us free will and will never force us to obey. He does not want us to be puppets but to love Him as He loves us. God has made us in His image, loving us even above the angels.

We see many examples in the Bible where God was patient beyond what we might have been. In Genesis, we read about Abraham begging God to save the city of Sodom, where his nephew and family live. He asks if 50 good people can be found in it, can the city be spared? But then it occurs to Abraham that there may be less than 50 good people, and he negotiates down to 40, then 30, then 20, then 10. Yet, still, that many good people can't be found. But God, who is merciful, understands Abraham's concern for his family and rescues his nephew and wife.

God's nature is just and loving; neither can be compromised. God has no ulterior motive or reason to be anything but. Each one of us can be sure of absolute fairness and justice. The Bible reminds us that we are all guilty of sin. *"Do not be deceived; God cannot be mocked. A man reaps what he sows. The one who sows to please his sinful nature, from that nature, will reap destruction. The one who sows to please God's Spirit, from the Spirit will reap eternal life."* (English Standard Version, The Bible, Galatians. 6.7-8)

As we discussed, no one measures up in their capacity. Therefore, we must depend on God's mercy and compassion, accepting His solution - salvation through faith in Jesus.

God takes no pleasure in punishment but must be faithful to His nature.

Personal Insights

A verse from the Bible is commonly used for posters and social media posts. It sums up God's true intention for us to escape punishment. He is a God who favors reconciliation and forgiveness.

"For God so loved the world, that he gave his only Son, that whoever believes in him should not perish but have eternal life." (English Standard Version, The Bible, John 3:16)

Jesus' death on the cross cancels out our sins. We were never meant to be separated from God. He wants us to be with Him eternally. But we cannot make this happen on our own. We must trust in God.

Over the past four chapters, we presented scientific evidence for God's existence, examined the main philosophical arguments, and then explored some historical evidence. We've looked at how our preconceived concept of God must shift to align with who He says He is. Now, we will examine how important faith is, how miracles show that we can trust God, how we approach God by praying, and the church's role in Christianity.

I would love to hear from you!

Through your support and reviews my book will be able to reach more people who are searching for reasons to believe. Please help me get it into their hands by taking 60 seconds to leave a review on Amazon. You can scan the code or connect at

https://www.amazon.com/review/create-review/?ie=UTF8&channel=glance-detail&asin=B0CK2ZSMCZ

Please follow these simple steps:

- Open Amazon on your phone
- Select the Camera in the Search Bar
- Hover it over the QR Code
- Rate/Review my book

Help others to trust in God!

CHAPTER 5

Essence of God

All that discussion about suffering and hell has probably left you wondering why so many people still believe in God. Is there any hope, any possibility of peace, and how do you discover joy? This chapter will be more lighthearted as we explore the nature of God and discuss how Jesus fits into God's plan for you. We will explore how God puts that plan into action through the Holy Spirit. Our focus turns from looking for evidence that God exists to who He is as a living person and how we can trust to Him.

Reason #14: The Nature of God

Besides the resurrection of Jesus, the core belief of Christianity is the Trinity of God the Father, Jesus Christ the Son, and the Holy Spirit. It is difficult to grasp how God can be three persons in one. We will never truly understand this concept while we are here on Earth. However, a little insight can help us understand how He relates to us and how we can relate to Him.

'Tri' means three, and 'unity' means one. Together, they make up the word Trinity, meaning three in one. Imagine a rope with three cords. Each cord (Father, Son, Holy Spirit) is the same. Entwined, they form one rope (Triune God).

The Father, Son, and Holy Spirit are distinct persons

The Bible is clear that each is a separate being or person: The Father *sent* the Son, indicating two different persons. The Holy Spirit was sent to the disciples when Jesus ascended into Heaven, indicating another person. Each person can speak, reason, think, understand, will, and feel. This distinction demonstrates each entity is real and not just three different roles or elements of one being. Jesus expressed this very clearly when He said, *"Go therefore and make disciples of all the nations, baptizing them in the name of the Father and the Son and the Holy Spirit."* (English Standard Version, The Bible, Matthew 28:19)

Each person of the Trinity is fully God and not just one-third God. God the Father is all God. The Son is all God. The Holy Spirit is all God. God is one essence but three distinct persons.

If each is a person, then are we talking about three Gods? No, absolutely not. The Bible is very clear on this point. *"[..a righteous God and a Savior; There's none besides me! Turn to me and be saved, all you ends of the Earth, For I am God, and there's no other ...]* (Common English Bible, Isaiah 45:21-22)

God the Father, the Son, and the Holy Spirit are three distinct Persons, each fully God, but only one God.

Is the Trinity Contradictory?

For something to be contradictory, it must disrupt the law of noncontradiction. Logically, A cannot be non-A. What 'is' cannot also be 'what it is not.' We cannot say that the sky is blue at 8 a.m. and then also say that the sky was not blue at 8 a.m. Either it was, or it wasn't blue at that particular time. It cannot be both. The same is true for the Trinity. God is not three and one in the same way, but He is three in a different way to which He is one. We do not deny that He is three by changing our minds to say He is one. He is three and one - He is God, not human like we are. God told Moses, *"I am who I am."* (English Standard Version, The Bible, Exodus 3:14)

Essence and Person

God is one in essence or being, but He is three in person. 'Essence' and 'person' are not the same thing. 'Essence' means the inherent nature or essential quality of something, which determines its character. God is only one being or essence. All three persons, Father, Son, and Spirit, are one essence or being. By 'person,' we do not mean three individuals that exist apart from each other. The three persons are not divided; they are one. The Bible tells us, *"For in Him (Jesus) the whole fullness of deity dwells bodily."* (English Standard Version, The Bible, Colossians 2:9)

Let's look at another Bible verse that refers to the Trinity. Jesus has just been baptized here, and the Father and the Holy Spirit express their pleasure with Him.

"And the Holy Spirit descended on him in bodily form, like a dove; and a voice came from Heaven, "You are my beloved Son; with you, I am well pleased." (English Standard Version, The Bible, Luke 3:22)

We see three persons in this scenario. The Son, coming out of the water, the Holy Spirit in the form of a dove, and the Father, not visible, but audible.

Personal Insights

Our knowledge of God is limited to what we know of our world. It is filtered through what we are taught or what we have experienced. Sometimes, our world makes understanding who God is and how He operates challenging. Here is where faith comes in to help. At some point, we must start believing and accepting that what the Bible teaches us about God is the truth. Then, as we get to know Him better, these concepts become more evident.

Here are a few examples of how you can get a grasp of who God is:

- In Isaiah 40, God is described as a Shepherd, tenderly gathering his lambs in his arms to comfort them.

- The same Chapter of the Bible describes Him as a magnificent God. He can hold all the water of the Earth in the hollow of His hand.

- He is a God who never changes - He is always the same, and we can, therefore, depend on Him (Hebrews 13:8).

- Jesus was loving and compassionate to people who were marginalized and rejected by society. There are many accounts in the Gospels.

- Jesus was also assertively opposed to the religious hypocritical leaders of his days who oppressed the people and put unjust laws and rules in place. He is our advocate.

- The book of Hebrews talks about Jesus as our High Priest who intercedes for us.

God is who He is: holy, righteous, and just. But He is also who I need Him to be: a loving Father, nurturing shepherd, provider, protector, and friend. In Hebrews, we are invited to approach God. *"Let us then with confidence draw near to the throne of grace, that we may receive mercy and find grace to help in time of need."* (English Standard Version, The Bible, Hebrews 4:16)

Having explored some of God's nature and who He is, discussing why there are so many different beliefs and religious options is important. Why do children grow up believing what they do? Why is it essential to seek the truth as we mature into adulthood?

Reason #15: Religious Diversity

Initially, children are exposed to the religious beliefs of their immediate family or community. Your parents' religion is what you adopt at first. However, our ability to travel broadly, broaden our knowledge via the internet, and be influenced by social media brings us into contact with other beliefs and religious diversity. There are both pros and cons to this. It means young people can explore different views and seek the truth for themselves. But it has also brought much confusion and opposition to those who have found the truth and adopted ideas that conflict with their immediate community. More than ever before, it is necessary to know what you believe and be able to expound on your belief.

There are three theories of religious diversity:

- The *pluralistic theory* holds that all religions are equally as good as each other.
- The *exclusivist theory* says that only one religion is relevant.
- The *inclusivist theory* takes the middle road, saying that one religion has the most value but agrees that all other religions also have significant value.

Religious Pluralism

The fact is that there has always been a diversity of religions. We see this in the Old Testament, where Israel was surrounded by nations that worshiped other gods and idols. They performed various religious practices that differed from what God taught them. We see religious diversity in the New Testament, where Jesus was born into Judaism yet challenged these beliefs with God's teachings and will. The early Christian church was surrounded by a culture steeped in Greek Philosophy, Roman paganism, and other religious beliefs. Since 'religious pluralism' has come to mean many things, varying from tolerance of other religions to suggestions that all religions are the same leading ultimately to God, we need to discuss what makes Christianity different from all other religions.

Is Christianity just one of many paths to God?

The confusion arises because people don't carefully examine who Jesus is before deciding the truth. Jesus claimed He is the only way to God. Is this a trustworthy claim?

What Makes Christianity Different?

Christianity is entirely different from other religions. It is not focused on our efforts to appease God and earn His approval through good deeds. It is focused on God making a way for *all* people to come to Him.

The Bible tells us that there is salvation only through Jesus.

"And there is salvation in no one else, for there is no other name under Heaven given among men by which we must be saved." (English Standard Version, The Bible Acts 4:12)

Isn't Christianity Like Any Other Religion?

No, it isn't. It is based on obedience and a relationship with a living God who can see, hear, and be present. Jesus is not just a prophet or a good man - He is the Son of God.

As Christians, our relationship grows in God and his love. Through this love, we want to share God with others. We try to follow in Jesus' footsteps by helping others, as Jesus showed in his life. He told his followers, *"A new commandment I give to you, that you love one another: just as I have loved you, you also are to love one another. By this, all people will know that you are my disciples if you have love for one another."* (English Standard Version, The Bible John 13:34-35)

These loving works are not a way to earn our way to Heaven. But Christians do them out of love, and we can pass them on because we receive love and acceptance from God.

The Resurrection

In chapter 3, when discussing the historical evidence, we looked at the biblical and non-biblical writings that point to the resurrection of Jesus. His body has never been found, despite extensive searches at the time of the early church and in later archaeological digs. He is indeed risen and alive - interested in our lives and eternal destiny.

Jesus' Claims About Himself:

- Jesus called God His Father, claiming that He did the same work as God. The religious leaders were so angry that they began to plot to kill Him. (John 5:17, 18)

- Jesus told his followers that He has the authority to forgive sin. This statement horrified the religious leaders because it is the same as claiming that He is God and, therefore, in their opinion, was blasphemy against God. (Mark 2:5 - 7)

- Jesus claimed He and the Father (God) are one. The leaders were so offended that they wanted to stone Him then and there. (John 10:30-33)

- Jesus claimed He would sit on the right hand of God. The leaders again said that He was blaspheming and ordered Him to be put to death. (Mark 14:61-64)

What distinguishes Christianity from other religions is that God is alive, and our salvation is gained through belief in Jesus and repentance for our sins. The Holy Spirit draws us to Him.

Personal Insights

"Jesus said to him, "I am the way, and the truth, and the life. No one comes to the Father except through me." (English Standard Version, the Bible John 14:6)

When I started college, I stopped attending church as I did prior to college. In the process I began to feel something was missing. So, I made myself attend on at least a semi-regular basis. It is hard when you are in college. At that time, my husband-to-be could do with or without attending church. His parents were not regular churchgoers. It wasn't until we started having kids that my husband thought about the impression that not attending church would leave on our children.

While at college, I enjoyed exploring various denominations with one of my friends. She introduced me to Christian rock music, and I have been hooked ever since. I took a religious class in college as well. I was curious and wanted to understand the differences between all the Christian denominations. Honestly, they are all similar. I realized we were all believers looking for the same outcome: spending eternity with God in Heaven. What a blessing it was to explore and learn as I did.

Your faith isn't about what denomination you are. Belief isn't about your church versus someone else's church's variations in service. Being a Christian is believing that Jesus came to Earth and died for our sins so we can spend eternity with Him in Heaven. Believing is about trusting that God is there for you no matter how good or bad you feel about your sins. He will forgive you if you believe and are sorry.

But, like all imperfect humans, we want more. We don't live at the time of Jesus. We have current-day miracles, but they are not shown in the news regularly, if at all. We have to search and find the truth for ourselves. My hope is you will find confidence in God's existence.

Having looked at who God is and how we need to approach Him, we will now focus on the role of faith, how faith changes lives and the power of prayer. We will look into miracles and whether they still happen today (and they do!). And we will close our discussion by exploring the role of the church.

CHAPTER 6

The Role of Faith

Something you may have picked up on throughout this book is that God does not think, act, or behave as humans. Nor does God always fit into our concept of who He is and how we should approach Him. The word 'faith' has cropped up several times. Although God sometimes relates to us practically and intellectually, we must approach Him through faith. The Bible is full of verses encouraging faith in God, in who He is, what He can do, and why He does things the way He does.

In this chapter, we will take an in-depth look at faith. We will investigate whether faith is sustainable by reason and evidence. We will discuss whether we can have faith without evidence or whether evidence is necessary for faith.

Reason #16: The Role of Faith

Whether faith and reason are compatible has sparked debate over the centuries. Some claim they are consistent, compatible, and harmonious, while others disagree.

For example, David Hume, the 18th-century philosopher, claimed that faith is contradictory to reason and firmly in the realm of the irrational. Roughly 100 years later, Soren

Kierkegaard, the 19th-century philosopher, emphasized faith over reason, but this tipped people's thinking to the point of irrationality. Calvin and Barth stated that faith exceeds reason and rational thought. They said using reason where faith is applied is inappropriate and irreverent.

Before Hume and Kierkegaard, the philosopher John Locke argued that faith and reason are compatible and rational, stating there is no conflict between the two concepts. He believed when reason is appropriately used and faith is correctly understood, they never contradict one another or compete.

Faith and reason are compatible and not contradictory to one another. This view was first expressed by the philosopher Thomas Aquinas and later confirmed by Pope John Paul II in 1998. In a letter to the Bishops, the Pope stated, *"Faith and Reason are like two wings on which the human spirit rises to the contemplation of truth."* He defended the importance of reason for any true believer and that faith and reason are not inconsistent but harmoniously work together. Faith is not contradictory to reason but requires reason and vice versa.

Thomas Aquinas, the thirteenth-century philosopher, stated faith in eternal salvation exhibits theological truth that transforms our reason. He said we could know religious truths without having faith. In other words, you can know God without believing in Him, though this would be an incomplete state. Aquinas thus separates rational (knowledge and reasoning) theology from revealed (God-given) theology.

The Bible talks about this in the Apostle Paul's second letter to Timothy, where he says many will constantly learn but never arrive at the truth. (2 Timothy 3:7) We need reason to read the Bible and to understand the truth, but we also need faith to accept these truths and to trust God.

Immanuel Kant, the eighteenth-century philosopher, wrote in "*The Conflict of the Faculties*" that divinely revealed truths are possible and knowable. He stated knowing the truth can also be for enlightenment and guidance, contributing to our moral improvement. Thus, Kant presents the concepts of reason and faith as working together in harmony.

The Benefits of Faith

- *Salvation*

Faith in Jesus brings us salvation. By repenting for our sins and trusting in God's forgiveness, we are saved from an eternity of separation from God. We cannot see what salvation will look like. We need faith that God's promise will become reality.

"God saved you by his grace when you believed. And you can't take credit for this; it is a gift from God. Salvation is not a reward for the good things we have done, so none of

us can boast about it. " (New Living Translation, The Bible Ephesians 2:8-9)

- *Strength*

Putting our faith in God brings the benefits that the Bible promises us. Life can be complicated, but God has promised to always be with those who trust Him. Knowing that we are not alone brings strength and courage.

"This is my command—be strong and courageous! Do not be afraid or discouraged. For the Lord your God is with you wherever you go. " (New Living Translation, The Bible Joshua 1:9)

- *Faith Gets Us to Act*

If we trust God by faith in salvation, we need to believe we are saved. The Amplified Bible puts it very well: *"Now faith is the assurance (title, deed, confirmation) of things hoped for (divinely guaranteed), and the evidence of things not seen [the conviction of their reality - faith comprehends as fact what cannot be experienced by the physical senses]. "* (The Amplified Bible, Heb 11:1)

Does this mean I can do as I wish, taking no responsibility for my behavior, and God will do the rest? No, it means that our actions match our faith. Here is an example from everyday life. As you enter the car at the beginning of your journey, you pray and ask for God's protection. By faith, you trust that you will get to your destination. But you are still responsible for fastening your seatbelt, driving at the lawful speed limit, stopping at the traffic lights, and obeying all the road rules.

This verse also helps us clarify that action follows faith:

"In view of all this, make every effort to respond to God's promises. Supplement your faith with a generous provision of moral excellence, and moral excellence with knowledge, and knowledge with self-control, and self-control with patient endurance, and patient endurance with godliness, and godliness with brotherly affection, and brotherly affection with love for everyone. The more you grow like this, the more productive and useful you will be in your knowledge of our Lord Jesus Christ." (The Living Translation, The Bible 2 Peter 1:5-8)

- *Faith Moves God to Act*

There are several examples in the Gospels where Jesus commended people for their faith and granted what they asked. Faith pleases God, and that moves Him to act on our behalf. God rewards our faith when we act in line with His will. Jesus rewarded the faith of a mother and a Centurion when they asked for the healing of their child and servant, respectively.

"What do you mean, 'If I can'?" Jesus asked. "Anything is possible if a person believes." (The Living Translation, The Bible, Mark 9:23)

- *Encourage Others*

As you read the Bible and your faith in God grows, you can help others by sharing what you have learned. It is encouraging for others to know you have been coping with something similar to what they may be going through. It is how we help one another. It will also help non-believers when they see your peace, joy, and strength.

Reason #17: The Choice of Faith

The Bible encourages us and shows us the benefits of faith. The choice is ours to believe. We can choose to take life on by ourselves, navigating its ups and downs, or we can choose to have faith in God, tapping into His resources, power, and wisdom for help. Faith in God requires us to believe He exists, rewarding those who trust Him.

There are many reasons why faith is essential. Some reasons to have faith benefit you directly, and some help those around you. Faith matters because:

- We have limited resources, but God can do the impossible
- Life is unpredictable, but God knows the future
- Faith brings hope and new possibilities
- Faith brings peace and calm
- Faith motivates us to do the right thing
- Faith helps us cope with difficult situations, such as losing a loved family member or friend

- Faith provides structure, regularity, and predictability
- Faith allows us to connect with a Being that is bigger than ourselves
- It helps us look inward and understand ourselves better

Consequences of Rejecting Faith

We have established that God is righteous and just, so choosing not to have faith has consequences. We read this in the book of Romans: "*For God in Heaven unveils his holy anger breaking forth against every form of sin, both toward ungodliness that lives in hearts and evil actions. For the wickedness of humanity deliberately smothers the truth and keeps people from acknowledging the truth about God.*" (The Passion Translation, The Bible, Romans 1:18)

- *Those who reject God get what they ask for*

Those who disregard God and choose to follow their own way will eventually find they are separated and far from God, bringing them to a dark and lonely place. We see this in the Old Testament with the Israelites - they wandered in the desert for 40 years because they refused to listen to God.

- *Those who reject God suffer unnecessarily*

Without faith in God, God will not intervene, which could mean those who choose not to put their trust in God suffer unnecessarily.

- *Those who reject God are left to their own devices*

Rejecting God means we do not rely on Him for any of the benefits He has promised to those who have faith in Him. Without His protection, provision, and direction, life can be chaotic.

Why Do We Have Free Will?

We discussed this in-depth previously, but since we have just looked at the consequences of not having faith, let's recap to get some perspective. Rather than creating us as pre-programmed puppets, God created us to think, reason, feel, and respond autonomously. In other words, He gave us free will. This does not mean we can do what we want without being held accountable or having consequences. We are responsible for the choices that we make. The Bible says, *"For whatever a man sows, that he will also reap. For he who sows to his flesh will of the flesh reap corruption, but he who sows to the Spirit will of the Spirit reap everlasting life."* (New King James Version, the Bible Galatians 6:7-8)

In the same way, God offers His gift of salvation, but the choice to put your faith in Him and accept it is entirely up to you. God wants you to accept Jesus, but the choice is yours.

There are many reasons to trust God, but these are perhaps the most common:

1. He knows better than we do

Because God is omniscient, He knows everything about you and your life, past, present, and future. Since He has this knowledge, He knows best what to do. If you connect with Him and allow Him to guide and lead you, you can tap into His wisdom to handle situations well. You can also avoid wrong decisions by following His lead. In the Bible, we read, *"If any of you lacks wisdom, let him ask God, who gives generously to all without reproach, and it will be given him. But let him ask in faith, with no doubting, for the one who doubts is like a wave of the sea that is driven and tossed by the wind."* (English Standard Version, The Bible, James 1:5 - 6)

2. All things are possible with Him

Throughout this book, we've discussed how God can do the impossible. Trust in God to do the impossible when a situation is beyond your control or anything you can do. Several times, Jesus told his followers that God can do the impossible. *"But he said, "What is impossible with man is possible with God."* (English Standard Version, The Bible, Luke 18:27)

3. He is worthy

Our trust is in God, who is not like us humans. He is trustworthy and faithful to what He has promised. He will not let you down or disappoint you. Even though He may not answer exactly as you want, He knows best and will come through for you. *"Trust in the LORD with all your heart. Never rely on what you think you know. Remember the LORD in everything you do, and he will show you the right way."* (Good News Bible, The Bible Proverbs 3:5-6)

4. He knows what He is doing

God has a purpose for your life, something unique that only you can do. If you trust Him, He will show you what it is and help you to achieve it. We read in Psalms, *"The Lord will fulfill his purpose for me; your steadfast love, Our Lord, endures forever. Do not forsake the work of your hands."* (English Standard Version, The Bible, Psalm 138:8)

5. Jesus is worth it

When I consider what it cost Jesus to ensure I can have freedom from sin and guilt, and receive forgiveness and all the benefits of faith - He is worth trusting.

Personal Insights

Putting our faith in God moves Him to fulfill His promises. Some of those promises are protection and a plan and purpose for our lives.

From an early age, I was drawn to God and felt God was asking me to do something big for Him. I felt a deep connection to God, especially after I would confess my sins.

It felt like I was clean and starting over again. I felt God was leading me to a deeper connection with Him.

At 15 years old, I was in my friend's car in the front seat but couldn't get the seatbelt to work. As she drove, the traffic light changed to red, but she didn't see it. We went straight into the side of a car crossing the road. We hit the car and slammed into a tree. I remember seeing a man with a beard and mustache looking through the driver's window. He was middle-aged with sandy brown hair. He looked at me and asked, "Are you okay?" I answered, "Yes."

The next thing I knew, I was waking up on my friend's lap in the driver's seat. My friend was still unconscious. The emergency trucks arrived. I asked the first person who came to the car, "Where is the man that was just here?" The emergency worker said they were the first on the scene. I said, "No, he was just here and asked if I was okay." The emergency worker looked around to see if he could find the man I described, but nobody was found.

My friend and I were checked at the scene and sent home with minor scrapes and bruises. Later, my friend told me the owner expressed sympathy when her car was taken to the junkyard. When she asked him why, he said the person in the passenger seat died at the scene. The windshield had been cracked where my head had hit. When the junkyard owner found out I wasn't even badly hurt, he couldn't believe it. He said he had never heard of someone living after hitting the windshield like I did.

God spared my life that day because I had chosen to put my faith in Him. My mom told me I won't die until I have fulfilled what God wants me to do here on Earth. She said that God still had plans for me.

God has a plan for you too, and although he gives us free will to choose to follow Him or not, if we do, He will fulfill that purpose and all His promises to you.

Reason #18: Faith Changes Lives

So, how does faith help us? Faith or belief is linked to the perception of life and its meaning. When you can attach importance to something, it becomes more valuable. When we perceive humans as valuable, we have more respect or regard for them. With a more profound sense comes purpose. When we find a purpose in our existence and what we do, we are more focused and more intentional in our actions.

Having a purpose is essential for mental health. Faith gives you something or someone to focus on, which provides structure to your life. The simple act of reading the Bible and praying each day can help ground you as a person. It gives hope, which is very important, especially if life is difficult or stressful. To be able to take your focus off the circumstances and to place it on God, who can help and do the impossible, is vital in keeping positive. Research done in Iran shows that using spiritual-religious psychotherapy in a group of mentally ill patients reduced depression and the frequency of suicidal thoughts.

The following aspects of faith and religion have a positive impact:

- *Community* - Holding a common faith provides social connections with others. This connection, in turn, creates a sense of belonging to the group in a safe and trustworthy environment.

- *Ritual* - Certain rituals help us to cope with difficult situations; for instance, a funeral or memorial allows us to bring closure and comfort when we lose a loved one. The performing of these rituals brings structure, predictability, and something to focus on at a time of overwhelming emotional upset. Observing certain days or special celebrations gives regularity and allows for time to rest.

- *Teachings* - provide a moral code or guideline to live or indicate right from wrong. Exercising compassion, forgiveness, and gratitude brings peace and harmony.

- *Individuality* - A sense of self develops as you connect with God, which also causes personal growth. When your sense of self is strong, you are more able to be accepting of others.

- *Mindfulness* - Reflection and meditation help to formulate a life outlook and philosophy.

- *Unity with surroundings* - This helps to develop a sense of belonging in the world and inspires awareness of your interaction with the physical environment.

Other Benefits of Faith

Health Benefits

Over 1,200 studies have shown a connection between faith and health. These benefits include avoiding illness as well as coping skills and quicker recovery. The research showed positive results for over 81% of those participating. Data from studies show that those involved in organized religion had a longer life expectancy of between seven and fourteen years. This benefit connects to more fulfilling relationships, especially marriage, and to healthier behaviors.

Mental Health

A study by the Royal College of Psychiatrists shows that faith has been able to slow psychosis. Ppatients involved in a supportive religious group have better insight and are more compliant with taking medication. In general, this is due to greater happiness and well-being. Faith provides hope and positivity, purpose and meaning to life, and greater support, all essential for mental health.

Coping With a Severe or Terminal Disease

Palliative care facilities recognize the benefits of faith in helping patients manage pain and distress. Due to the well-being factors discussed previously, they found that terminal patients retain hope and are less distressed. They also sleep more restfully and have less anxiety.

This positive link between faith and health can be attributed to the following factors:

- *Mental outlook* - Faith bolsters attitudes and expectations, and answers existential questions. A study showed that hopelessness is a risk factor for heart attacks and cancer, which increase the death rate even in healthy individuals. Lower anxiety means lower blood pressure and cholesterol. Faith brings hope in even the direst of circumstances.

- *Positive health care* - Faith brings greater morality and reduces risky behavior. There is generally lower alcohol consumption, less smoking and drug use, and less permissive sexual behavior among those with faith.

- *Social relationships* - Greater stability in family relationships, particularly marriages, is found in those regularly attending religious meetings.

- *Immunity* - Many studies have linked the interaction of the brain and a positive mental state to increased immunity. It lowers cortisol levels and reduces inflammation markers, lowering infection rates. A study on HIV patients who embraced faith after their diagnosis showed significantly less decline in CD4 counts and a slower disease progression.

- *Divine intervention* - Various studies have shown the outcome of intercessory prayer on health results. Improvements have been demonstrated in health outcomes.

Neuroscience researchers have found that faith is a natural byproduct of how our brains work. We are driven to find order where there is chaos and make sense of the world around us. Because of this, religion has been a part of human history for centuries. Doctor of Psychology Justin Barratt states that people are biased toward the supernatural, and even children as young as three attribute these abilities to God. This bias is irrespective of whether they have any teaching about God or not. He says, *"What we're showing is that our basic cognitive equipment biases us toward certain kinds of thinking and leads to thinking about a pre-life, an afterlife, gods, invisible beings that are doing things — themes common to most of the world's religions."*

Faith works because of who God is - He can do the impossible. Including faith in your everyday life will impact everything. Think about what happens when you throw a stone into a lake. The ripple effect from where it lands is similar to how faith will permeate and ripple through your life.

Here are some examples:

- *Worry into prayer* - Use your anxious thoughts to formulate a prayer directed to God, who hears when you call on Him.

- *Fear into courage* - Fear is a powerful emotion that can immobilize us. But when we pray and ask God to help, we are reminded of the many times God told people in the Bible to have courage and not to fear because He would be with them. He has promised to be with you.

- *Mistakes into growth* - We prefer to avoid making mistakes. Bad decisions or wrong actions do not need to haunt you. You can ask God for forgiveness, ask others for forgiveness, and then ask God to help you get it right. *"Put off your old self, which belongs to your former manner of life and is corrupt through deceitful desires, and to be renewed in the spirit of your minds, and to put on the new self, created after the likeness of God in true righteousness and holiness. (English Standard Version, The Bible, Ephesians 4:22-24)*

- *Stronger connections in relationships* - Relationships are undermined when we lack self-esteem or hang onto past hurts and bitterness. Asking God to help you let go and learning to grow helps to improve relationships with friends, family, coworkers, and neighbors.

- *Conversations into compassion* - Faith motivates us to act as our hearts are changed. As you talk to others, you will become aware of their needs and struggles, and then you can ask God to help you act with kindness or practical assistance. *"And I will give you a new heart, and a new spirit I will put within you. And I will remove the heart of stone from your flesh and give you a heart of flesh." (English Standard Version, The Bible, Ezekiel 36:26)*

- *Anger released to God* - It's easy to get angry when things don't go how you want them to. Trusting God to work out a situation means you can step back, take a deep breath, and respond rather than react.

- *Doubt into preparation* - We all face challenges, and only some are confident enough to tackle the unknown. When you trust God and are sure that He wants the best outcome for you, you can ask Him for wisdom to prepare and face those challenges better equipped.

- *Complaining into gratitude* - Faith provides hope, and a hopeful outlook on life helps you to be more positive and see the reasons to be grateful.

- *Judgment into reflection* - Understanding God's mercy and grace leads to less judgment of yourself and others and helps you to reflect rather than criticize.

- *Self-focus into Christ-focus* - As we grow in faith, our focus turns to God and less on ourselves, making us less self-absorbed and more open to caring for others.

Reason #19: The Evidence of Miracles

Let's clarify what we mean by 'miracle.' According to the dictionary, 'miracle' means an extraordinary and welcome event that cannot be explained by natural or scientific laws and can, therefore, be attributed to the intervention of a divine being.

From the above definition, we see that miracles have conceptual and epistemological aspects:

The *conceptual aspect* focuses on a miracle being an infringement of natural law. In other words, it is an event that occurs outside of natural laws. It also presents the dilemma of whether a miracle occurred due to some natural law that we don't yet know about, or did it occur due to divine intervention.

Epistemology focuses on attributing the miracle to divine intervention because it cannot have overstepped natural law.

The Nature of Miracles

Many events described in the Bible are outside the processes of usual physical laws as we know them. But sometimes, God uses nature in an unusual way to perform a miracle. God can perform miracles within the customary laws of nature, but it's also possible God does miracles stretching beyond nature's laws. In Exodus, we read how God used the wind to hold back the water of the Red Sea so the people could cross through on dry land. God stopped holding the water back to prevent their enemies from catching up to the Israelites. Another example is when Joshua, leader of Israel, asked God to stop the sun's rotation during a battle. (Joshua 10:12) Do we have proof of this event?

"The researchers developed a new eclipse code, which takes into account variations in the Earth's rotation over time. From their calculations, they determined that the only annular eclipse visible from Canaan between 1500 and 1050 BC was on 30 October 1207 BC, in the afternoon. Independent evidence that the Israelites were in Canaan between 1500 and 1050 BC can be found in the Merneptah Stele." (From *The Times of Israel* by David Sedley, 30 October 2017, 10:11 pm)

The laws of nature do not bind God in the same way they bind us. God can work within the same laws He set up for us, but sometimes, He chooses to work outside those laws.

Buckley

L.A.

To say that miracles do not occur is to claim that we know everything, which we don't.

The Resurrection of Christ

The resurrection of Jesus Christ is an example of where God ignored the natural law of our universe. Usually, when a person dies, their body becomes lifeless and begins to decay. But three days after Jesus died, God chose to show His incredible power by raising Jesus to life again. We examined the evidence to prove this miracle and the objections raised in Chapter 3, Reason #10. All the suggestions trying to explain why this occurred can be refuted. The Resurrection of Jesus could only have been done supernaturally by God. Despite extensive searching, the remains of Jesus' body have never been found.

The Parting of the Red Sea

Earlier, we mentioned this example briefly. Let's examine it more closely. The Israelites fled from their oppressors in Egypt and were trapped between the edge of the Red Sea and the Egyptian army. God held back the water so His people could continue to the land of Canaan. Critics have tried to explain away this miracle by proposing the event occurred elsewhere, in a shallow marsh of reeds. Others have proposed a strong wind of more than 70 miles per hour could have driven back the water, and when it died down, the water rushed back in. However, these proposed variations don't match the Biblical data. The Bible records state all of Pharoah's army drowned. Chariots, horses, and well-trained soldiers could not have drowned in a shallow marsh. The Bible clearly describes water piled up on *both* sides of the Israelites as they passed through. For this to happen, God had to cause the wind to blow in two opposite directions at the same place and time. In this miracle, God controlled the natural phenomenon of wind in a way that defies natural laws.

Jesus Walks on Water

Three of four Gospel writers tell us about Jesus walking on water in a storm. They all specify that the boat was far out, John telling us the distance of about three or four miles. This information refutes the rebuttal that Jesus was walking along the shore, and the disciples mistook Him walking on the water. The account in the Gospel also tells us there was a storm, indicating that the sea was rough and the wind was blowing strongly. The storm negates the proposition that Jesus was standing in a small boat, and the disciples missed this detail in the scenario. Surfers will tell us that standing on any surface is impossible without being thrown over when the winds and the seas are rough. Putting these facts together indicates this was a miracle.

We also read that Jesus encourages Peter to step out of the boat and join Him. While Peter trusted Jesus he could also walk on the water. But the moment Peter looked at the raging sea, he lost focus on Jesus. Peter'is faith was undermined and he began to sink, needing Jesus to rescue him.

Natural laws and the details of the events refute all the opposition against these miracles. God is the creator of the universe, and He set natural laws to bring order and govern it. God can also overrule the laws of nature and exercise power over these laws when He chooses.

We read of many healing miracles that Jesus performed while He was on Earth:

- At a wedding in Cana, to spare the hosts embarrassment, Jesus turned water into wine. The wine provided tasted better than what was initially served. (John 2: 1 - 12)

- A man blind from birth sees for the first time after Jesus touches his eyes. (Mark 8:22-26)

- Jesus takes two fish and five small loaves of bread, blesses them, and over 5000 people eat. Twelve baskets of leftovers are collected after the meal. (Mark 8:4 - 10)

- A man paralyzed from birth gets up and walks after Jesus tells him his sins are forgiven. (Matthew 9:1–8)

- A woman who has spent all her money on doctors to try and get well touches the hem of Jesus' clothes and goes home completely healed. (Luke 8:43- 48)

These are just a few of the many miracles that Jesus performed. The early church Apostles also performed miracles in the name of Jesus. We read about these miracles in the book of Acts in the Bible.

Why Don't We See Miracles Like the Apostles Did?

Although no longer as ordinary, there are also many accounts of miracles done today. But modern-day skepticism in miracles can be traced back to the eighteenth century. Professor of Theology Gottfried Less wrote a book called *Wahrheit der Christlichen Religion* in 1758. His theory is that to establish the validity of a miracle, one must first confirm the event did actually occur and then resolve the miraculous character of the event. This theory resulted in the disintegration of the credibility of miracles in the Gospel within theological circles. Thus began a trend in the early 1800s to explain away miracles described in the Gospels. There have been many who opposed these theories, but also many who added to them, further confusing the debate. To get a deeper understanding, let's examine what purpose these Gospel miracles served.

The Purpose of Miracles in Scripture

Miracles performed by God and Jesus were to show God's sovereign power over natural laws and the supernatural. These miracles were evidence of God Himself. They gave authenticity to God's message through His chosen messenger. In the Old Testament, God's messengers were prophets. In the New Testament, God's messenger was Jesus, His only son. Then, later, the Apostles of the early church.

In the Old Testament, miracles show God's authority over the universe. Jesus told us the purpose of miracles is to show God's sovereignty. In the New Testament, miracles performed by Jesus show us His divine identity. Miracles performed by the Apostles in the early church revealed the presence of the Holy Spirit, who was sent after Jesus ascended to Heaven. These miracles proved Jesus' resurrection and man's eternal destination.

The Bible gives us some indication of the purpose of miracles. *"What Jesus did here in Cana of Galilee was the first of the signs through which he revealed his glory and his disciples believed in him."* (New International Version, The Bible, John 2:11). It is clear that Jesus performed miracles to show his divine identity and prove his credibility as the Son of God.

Miracles Today

God intended for miracles to continue. The Bible encourages us to trust God for the 'impossible' and declares that there is nothing too complicated for Him to do. Miracles are not always significant, spectacular events. We must expand our understanding of how God works. Sometimes, He works in stunning displays, and sometimes, He sends a simple answer to a quiet, whispered prayer.

Jesus told his disciples they would do greater works than Him. There has been much debate about whether Jesus was referring to more miracles or more spectacular miracles. The Biblical Scholar D.A. Carson gives us some insight with this quote: "*Greater works . . . cannot simply mean more works—i.e., the church will do more things than Jesus did, since it embraces so many people over such a long time—since there are excellent Greek ways of saying "more," and since in any case the meaning would then be unbearably trite. Nor can greater works mean "more spectacular" or "more supernatural" works: it is hard to imagine works that are more spectacular or supernatural than the raising of Lazarus from the dead, the multiplication of bread, and the turning of water into wine.*" (D. A. Carson, *The Gospel According to John*, Pillar New Testament Commentary (Grand Rapids, MI: Eerdmans, 1991), 495)

The 'greater works' point to miracles happening against Jesus' death, resurrection, and ascension, giving the Gospel message validity and showing evidence that He is the Son of God. What the Apostles began was spreading the news of Jesus throughout the lands. The conversion to Christianity and belief in Jesus Christ will bring salvation to many.

God's plan for salvation reaches all people. We know this because miracles happened to people from various nationalities, not only the local people from Jerusalem. The purpose of miracles in the current-day church should include the forgiveness of sin. God's Plan of Redemption is as miraculous as physical healing, signs, and wonders. God is still active today in calling people to Himself, answering prayers, doing what we can't accomplish, stepping in when we are overwhelmed, and encouraging us to trust Him.

Personal Insights

A friend tells this account of a miracle: Her eight-year-old daughter fell and hurt her left knee. Two days later, the knee was still sore so she took the girl to the doctor to get it checked. The doctor said the cartilage in the knee was likely torn. He was concerned because this type of injury does not quickly repair itself, and since the child loved sports, he wanted to prevent her from having trouble with it in the future. The doctor referred them to an orthopedic surgeon.

The surgeon confirmed the cartilage was torn. He did an MRI, magnetic resonance image, to see exactly where and how bad of an injury. The MRI clearly showed the tear. The child was booked for surgery two days later to repair the damage. That evening, at a Bible study group, people prayed for the eight-year-old girl to be healed 100% with no future trouble.

The surgery went as planned. The sugeon spoke to the parents after the child came out of the operating room. Three of his colleagues were with him: the anesthetist, the assisting surgeon, and the nurse. He was white-faced as he said, "I sincerely apologize, but we have just done a completely unnecessary surgery. I do not understand. The MRI clearly shows a tear in the left meniscus." The sugeon asked the parents to confirm it was the left knee, which they did. He pulled out the MRI to show them there had been a tear. He pointed to the label showing the left knee. "But now, when we wanted to repair the cartilage, we found a pristine white, completely intact cartilage on her left knee. There is no sign of any injury ever having been there. There is no scar tissue." The surgeon proceeded to show them an image of the left knee taken in the operating room to confirm there wasn't a tear. He said, "I have never seen or heard of a torn cartilage repairing spontaneously, and certainly not in two days."

What a miracle! The girl is now 23 years old and leads an entirely active life, doing daily cardio, running, hiking, going to the gym, and doing squats without any trouble with her knee.

God still does miracles even when we least expect them.

CHAPTER 7

Prayer and Religion

At this point, I hope you are convinced that God is real. You may think, if God is real and Jesus saved us from our sins, I'm good. Why are you writing about prayer? I don't need to pray; you just gave me the reasons to believe. I definitely don't want to go to a service! Why does this have anything to do with trusting in God?

I understand these thoughts. Covid had me staying at home. I rarely participated in service even though it was being streamed. I felt okay about it. Plenty of people still believe and don't attend church.

I also thought I was praying enough and in the correct way. I thought of God often - when I looked at the majestic trees and sang Christian songs on the radio as a form of prayer. So, I'm good, right? Well, I quickly learned that I wasn't good.

Reason #20: The Power of Prayer

During the pandemic, you may have experienced depression and uncertainty. Many people found themselves praying to God for comfort and peace. Phycologists did a study on our response to prayer. They found online prayer searches rose 9.2% in January and February of 2020 and 29% in March and April. This trend continued throughout 2020, averaging 11% higher than the previous two years. The data was retrieved from Google searches done in over 107 countries. The Google figures for March 2020 reached the highest ever.

The Science of Prayer

Dr. Andrew Newberg, co-author of the book *How God Changes Our Brain: Breakthrough Findings From a Leading Neuroscientist,* states believing in God's existence is fundamentally good for us as humans. Newberg has pinpointed several effects that prayer has on the brain. The neural circuit is strengthened, enhancing our social awareness and empathy. In return, we can suppress negative emotions and heighten our sense of compassion.

Our brains are flexible or neuroplastic. They continue to develop based on our everyday experiences. If we engage in positive actions and behaviors, our brain changes, becoming independent of memories. Thus, praying can help to reduce memories of bad or negative experiences.

Prayer helps to maintain a healthy balance in life. Newberg, who has admitted he is unsure whether God exists, sees the scientific evidence of the benefits and encourages daily prayer with personal reflection.

New research shows prayer and meditation release feel-good chemicals into your brain. Praying and meditating are highly effective in curbing our reactions to trauma and adverse events. Dr. David Spiegel, associate chair of psychiatry and behavioral sciences and the medical director of the Center for Integrative Medicine at Stanford University School of Medicine, says, *"Praying involves the deeper parts of the brain: the medial prefrontal cortex and the posterior cingulate cortex — the mid-front and back portions. These parts of the brain are involved in self-reflection and self-soothing."* We can see this in an MRI. When the reflective part of the brain is engaged, the activity part of the brain is dormant.

The NYU Langone Medical Center did a study with volunteers from members of Alcoholics Anonymous. During an MRI, members were shown images of drinking or alcoholic drinks to stimulate cravings. Then they prayed, and the cravings were reduced. The MRI data shows changes in the prefrontal cortex which controls emotions.

Another study demonstrated when we are under stress, people having a natural reaction to 'fight' remained calmer and less active when they prayed. Dr. Paul Hokemeyer, a marriage, family, and addictions therapist, explains, *"Prayer and meditation are highly effective in lowering our reactivity to traumatic and negative events. They are powerful because they focus our thoughts on something outside ourselves."*

Prayer is about trust - trusting in God. God promises when we call on Him, He will answer. He is sovereign. But sometimes it doesn't feel like answers are coming through. It's like the dynamics between a responsible parent and an immature child. The child makes demands that the parent knows will neither be beneficial nor helpful. Giving in to the child's demands will be destructive or prevent an essential lesson. Let's look at how God answers us with our best interests at heart.

Five Ways God Answers Prayers

- *Yes*

God is able and willing to answer our prayers with an immediate 'yes' if that is what's best for us. You will often find that God responds quickly and decisively to intervene on your behalf. But an immediate yes is usually not observed.

- *No*

Like any good and responsible parent, there are times when God says 'No.' For us, this isn't easy to understand. We do not see the future or always have all the facts. We must trust that when God says no, He is sparing us trauma, has something better, or knows something that we don't. He always acts in our best interest - we have to trust Him.

- *Wait*

We want instant answers because we live in a fast-paced and instant world. God is an intentional God with a purpose for everything. Sometimes, we need to develop character and patience. If God makes you wait, He is preparing something more significant for you. This verse says it well, *"What no one ever saw or heard, what no one ever thought could happen, is the very thing God prepared for those who love him."* (Good News Bible, The Bible, 1 Corinthians 2:9)

- *Here's an alternative*

Sometimes circumstances are beyond our control, or things happen that we did not plan or even want. If we trust God and submit to His plan, we will look back and see that He had a better plan.

- *Yes, and...*

Sometimes, my prayers were small and focused on only the essentials because I did not trust God enough. Then God answered them and gave me much more than I ever dreamed.

How to Pray Effectively

There is no set formula for getting God to answer our prayers. Praying develops a personal relationship with God. He hears our prayers if we come to Him in sincerity and faith. Here are some suggestions to help you focus your prayers.

Concentration

Since prayer is a conversation with God, eliminating distractions is essential. Suppose you were talking to your friend on the phone. You should focus on the conversation. If you couldn't, you'd deal with the distraction by moving to another room, choosing a quiet moment when the family was out and about, closing the door to the room, and so on. Removing distractions helps to focus on talking to God.

Importance of meditation

One of the best ways to pray is defined through scripture. If you pray according to God's ways, you will likely connect with Him. It's like finding common interests to build a relationship. Take time to read verses in the Bible and meditate, think, mull over them, asking the Holy Spirit to show you what they mean.

Perseverance

Keep going until you get an answer. Keep talking to God, discussing various aspects of the problem with Him. Even though He is all-knowing, He loves you and wants to connect and build a relationship. Prayer helps develop your relationship with God.

Submit to His will

The primary purpose of prayer is not to move God's hand but to be changed by the Holy Spirit. Put your trust in God - He loves you and wants the best for you. Mother Teresa said, *"I used to believe that prayer changes things, but now I know that prayer changes us, and we change things."* (Is prayer changing things? - Foundations with Janet Denison. https://www.foundationswithjanet.org/blog/is-prayer-changing-things/)

Types of Prayer and Their Purpose

Any time you talk to God, you are praying. Understanding some of the terms used in the Bible and formal religion will help.

- *Supplication*

Supplication is a method of asking, petitioning, or making our requests and needs known. It is, however, only one facet of prayer. If we use only supplication for prayer, we will miss out on what God has in store for us. It's like going to an ATM to make a withdrawal - routine and mundane.

- *Thanksgiving*

With this type of prayer, we express gratitude or acknowledge that God is the giver of good gifts. We all have something we can be grateful for - essentials, home comforts, family, friends, a job, etc. Having a grateful and positive attitude helps us to approach God more readily.

- *Adoration*

When we consider who God is and what He has done for us, expressing our love to God is appropriate. Reading through the book of Psalms in the Bible will help you to find the words to adore God.

- *Confession*

The Holy Spirit helps convict us of our wrongdoing. When you become aware of sin or transgression, confess your mistake to God. Ask Him for forgiveness. Accept that He does forgive: *"But if we confess our sins to God, he will keep his promise and do what is right: he will forgive us our sins and purify us from all our wrongdoing."* (The Good News Bible, The Bible 1John 1:9)

Then, ask God for help to overcome and do right in the future.

- *Intercession*

This type of prayer is for others or asking God to intervene on their behalf. Many people will tell you they didn't pray but experienced answers or miracles because someone else was praying for them.

Above all, come to God as you are. He knows your heart. Don't be afraid to approach God. Prayer is powerful not because of how we pray but because of who God is.

Reason #21: The Role of the Church

In the creation account, we see as far back as Genesis that God did not intend humans to be alone. He designed us to be happiest in the community - families, groups of friends, like-minded people with similar interests, and so on. It's about challenging life together and enriching our inner beings. 'Church' is the community that provides Christians with encouragement and support. But it's also there to ensure that we grow in our faith. There is a renewed desire for community and in-person contact after we could not meet during the pandemic.

How Is Community God's Design for Growth?

- *A way to see Christ in others*

Faith in God is to follow Jesus and develop the attributes or characteristics He displayed. We will feel His love, presence, forgiveness, and healing in a community embracing the same desire. In this harsh world, the church is a respite surrounded by compassion, encouragement, and strength.

- *A source of accountability and guidance*

The church is where we can teach and grow in our faith. We share our experiences and learn from each other. Even the most experienced person can learn from someone new in the faith who has fresh eyes. Someone else may have navigated the same situation and can offer guidance or advice. This is how we grow. The church community provides a source of accountability. Often, it is easier to overcome something if we are accountable to others for our actions.

- *A place to pray and worship*

A community joined in prayer is compelling. We pray as a community for one another and our world. The church is a place that provides the space to worship God. Whether this is with music, scripture, or quiet reflection, we can focus our attention on worshipping collectively. Feeling this connection to others who believe as you believe gives comfort and safety.

- *A place to serve*

Community is where we turn our attention off ourselves and onto others. We share the talents and abilities that God has given us by serving others. The Bible likens the church community to a human body. The ear has a different function from the foot, which operates differently from the hand or the eye. Each person in the community has a different role or set of skills that can be used to benefit others. Sometimes, we can share material possessions if others lack them, but a simple smile or listening ear can go a long way in helping others. There are many ways to help. Maybe your talent is building a ramp. You could help a single mom transport her children to after-school practices. Having tea with a lonely retiree is another way to serve. The possibilities are endless.

- *A witness to the world*

The sense of community and love shared among Christians can be very powerful. It helps draw people into the church. We help people believe by sharing our faith with others. Others can see something special and want to learn what draws them to you. It's as if God's light is shining through you. You are giving yourself as a witness to others just as the church gives witness to the world.

- *Ambassador of God's love*

God's love embraces all people. His heart is toward reconciliation and healing. The church community can reflect this to all people. God's love can be shown in many ways, such as feeding the hungry, donating goods to the less fortunate, sharing the love of Jesus with those who don't attend church, etc. Each of these methods of reaching out helps to build God's church.

- *Function over form*

The church is not about function or structure - it's about relationships. Relationships are to strengthen, encourage, and love. Community provides these essentials as we face the challenges of life.

- *Getting small*

The early church was made of small groups gathering for personal interaction. They were without builds or funds, so they met in homes to worship, pray, and teach scripture. Everyone had something to offer: instruction, a song, a prayer, or a revelation. Within a large church, joining a smaller group will help personalize your involvement. It is about participation that meets your needs or the needs of others.

- *A call to community*

The purpose of a community is to live out our faith as we connect with others. It isn't just a once-a-week event but a continual daily interaction with others to share in God's love and Jesus for the forgiveness of our sins.

Why Worship Matters

Worship is more than just singing a few songs in church. It is a lifestyle of practicing our faith and celebrating who Jesus is daily.

The Bible gives us information about the type of worship that pleases God. *"So then, my friends, because of God's great mercy to us, I appeal to you: Offer yourselves as a living sacrifice to God, dedicated to his service and pleasing to him. This is the true worship that you should offer."* (The Good News Bible, The Bible, Romans 12:1) It's no longer about me and what I want, but about what God wants for me.

True worship is about honoring God. We need to read the Bible to find out what pleases Him and how we should behave. But it's also about talking to God by praying and asking Him for personal insight into your life. Let God shape your thoughts, opinions, and attitude.

Sacrifice is a part of believing. It's easy to express praise and gratitude when things are going well. But it takes faith to be grateful when things are not going as you would like. Therefore, we must continue worshipping when we face pain and loss. Worship helps us move towards God. Otherwise, we may miss His love and help.

There is an excellent example in the Book of Acts. Paul and Silas are in pain. They are in an awful circumstance, yet they praise God despite their situation. Around midnight, beaten and chained, Paul and Silas were praying and singing hymns of praise. Suddenly, there was an earthquake - the ground shook, and the prison gates flew open.

This experience resulted in the disciples sharing the Gospel of salvation with the guard and his family. The Magistrate released Paul and Silas. You can read the entire story in Acts 16:25 - 34. Worshipping God can change your circumstances.

Worship helps us focus less on ourselves and our circumstances and puts our focus on God. God can do the impossible. God knows us more intimately than we know ourselves. He wants what's best for us.

Conclusion

I hope some of your questions have been answered and you found this thought-provoking. Scientific evidence points to God's existence as the Creator and designer of our universe. We see this in the intricately designed details. We established that the universe has a starting point. We went back and forth with philosophical arguments and issues raised over centuries. We found value in moral, ontological, cosmological, and teleological debates about God's existence. The moral code that motivates some to do right, while others ignore it and do wrong, was instilled in us since the beginning of time. It shapes our behavior and points to a righteous and just God.

We explored what happens to those who choose to ignore God's direction. The Gospel writers gave us historical accounts of Jesus' life, which have been backed up and collaborated by other writings from around the same period. Archeological finds confirm many of the details. Jesus performed many miracles, proving Him to be the Son of God, part of the Trinity, yet one God of the universe.

One of the greatest miracles of all time, the Resurrection, validates Christianity. It sets it apart from all other religions - a living God who hears our prayers, answers our cries, and longs for a relationship. God gave us free will by which we choose to place our faith in Him. We offer our hearts in worship. He is a God of restoration, reconciliation, and enduring love.

Faith is essential for facing the challenges of life. We explored the physical benefits of faith and ways to put our faith into action. There are benefits of community and power in prayer. Like most things in life, we don't know everything. You will grow and learn much more by reading your Bible, connecting with people who base their faith on God's word, praying, and worship. It's a lifelong journey of discovery.

If you have not yet put your faith and trust in God, read the Bible - the Gospels are a good place to start. Pray by talking to God about everything and ask Him to reveal Himself to you in a way you fully understand. Then, look for a community of people who share God's word, getting involved by putting your faith into action.

I would love to hear from you!

Through your support and reviews my book will be able to reach more people who are searching for reasons to believe. Please help me get it into their hands by taking 60 seconds to leave a review on Amazon. You can scan the code or connect at

https://www.amazon.com/review/create-review/?
ie=UTF8&channel=glance-detail&asin=B0CK2ZSMCZ

Please follow these simple steps:

- Open Amazon on your phone
- Select the Camera in the Search Bar
- Hover it over the QR Code
- Rate/Review my book

Help others to trust in God!

Sources

(2001). *What Does the Bible Say About Holy.* Open Bible.

https://www.openbible.info/topics/holy(2021). *20 Best Bible Verses About Miracles.* Bible Study Tools.

https://www.biblestudytools.com/topical-verses/bible-verses-about-miracles/

(2016). *The Mental Health Benefits of Religion and Spirituality.* National Alliance on Mental Illness.

https://www.nami.org/Blogs/NAMI-Blog/December-2016/The-Mental-Health-Benefits-of-Religion-Spiritual

(2021). *Scientific Proof of God.* All About Creation.

https://www.allaboutcreation.org/scientific-proof-of-god-faq.htm

(2022-23). *Quotes from Mother Teresa.* Glowscotland.
https://blogs.glowscotland.org.uk/ed/turnbullvva/quotes-from-mother-teresa/

(2023). *Alvin Plantinga's Free Will Defense.* Wikipedia.

https://en.wikipedia.org/wiki/Alvin_Plantinga%27s_free-will_defense

(2023). *Problem of Hell.* Wikipedia.

https://en.wikipedia.org/wiki/Problem_of_Hell

(2023). *The Ontological Argument: Existence as Perfection.* Academy 4SC.

https://academy4sc.org/video/the-ontological-argument-existence-as-perfection/#:~:text=The%20ontological%20argument%20says%20that,%3B%20therefore%2C%20it%20must%20exist.

(2023). *Transcendental Argument for the Existence of God.* Wikipedia.

https://en.wikipedia.org/wiki/Transcendental_argument_for_the_existence_of_God

Alcorn, R. (2019). *Why is the Resurrection so Important?* Bible Study Tools.

https://www.biblestudytools.com/bible-study/topical-studies/why-is-the-resurrection-so-important.html

Ames, R. (2005). *Seven Proofs of God's Existence.* Tomorrows World.

https://www.tomorrowsworld.org/magazines/2005/may-june/seven-proofs-of-gods-existence?

Armand, M. (2021). *How Does Faith Impact Your Life? 10 Examples of How Faith Changes Everything.* Butterfly Living.

https://butterflyliving.org/how-does-faith-impact-your-life/

Azar, B. (2010). *A Reason to Believe.* American Psychological Association.

https://www.apa.org/monitor/2010/12/believe

Bartels, M., Rosa-Aquino, P., & Guenot, M. (2023). *25 of the Most Mind-Boggling Phenomena on Earth Business.* Insider.

https://www.businessinsider.com/25-of-the-coolest-natural-phenomena-2016-6

Basis for Objective Moral Values. TGC Canadian Edition.

https://ca.thegospelcoalition.org/article/gods-existence-basis-objective-moral-values/

Beebe, G. (2012). *How Faith and Prayer Benefit the Brain.* Westmont Magazine.

https://www.westmont.edu/how-faith-and-prayer-benefit-brain#:~:text=When%20we%20intently%20and%20consistently,maintain%20and%20even%20restore%20community

Beebe, J.R. (ISSN 2161-0002*). Logical Problem of Evil.* Internet Encyclopedia of Philosophy.

https://iep.utm.edu/evil-log/

Benjamin, B. (2008). *Creation and Intelligent Design: God v god.* Answers in Genesis.

https://answersingenesis.org/intelligent-design/creation-and-intelligent-design-god-vs-god/

Bentzen, J. (2021). *In crisis, we pray: Religiosity and the COVID-19 pandemic.* National Library of Medicine.

https://www.ncbi.nlm.nih.gov/pmc/articles/PMC8557987/#:~:text=The%20estimates%20document%20that%20average,to%20the%20two%20previous%20years.

Bhawanie, E.D. (2018). *Classical Arguments for the Existence of God.* Research Center for Apologetics.

https://www.csmedia1.com/317ministries.net/classical-arguments-for-the-existence-of-god.pdf

Bricker, S. (2022). *What is the Significance of Worship?* Christianity.com.

https://www.christianity.com/wiki/church/what-is-the-significance-of-worship.html

Broussard, K. (2021). *The Reliability of the Gospels.* Catholic Answers.

https://www.catholic.com/magazine/print-edition/the-reliability-of-the-gospels

Bunn, A. & Randall, D. (2011). *Health Benefits of Christian Faith.* The Human Journey.

https://humanjourney.org.uk/articles/health-benefits-of-christian-faith/

Burns, J. (2023). *6 Reasons We Can Believe in the Resurrection of Jesus Christ - Your Daily Bible Verse April 18.* Crosswalk.com.

https://www.crosswalk.com/devotionals/your-daily-bible-verse/6-reasons-we-can-believe-in-the-resurrection-of-jesus-christ-bible-study-minute-april-6-2018.html

Carson, D. A. (1991) *The Gospel According to John.* Pillar New Testament Commentary. http://www.amazon.com/Gospel-according-Pillar-Testament-Commentary/dp/0802836836/?tag=thegospcoal-20

Chaput, C. (2013). *Why Faith Matters: Belief as a Cornerstone of What it Means to be Human.* Catholic Philly.com.

https://catholicphilly.com/2013/08/homilies-speeches/why-faith-matters-belief-as-a-cornerstone-of-what-it-means-to-be-human/

Copan, P. (2016). *Prove to Me That God Exists: Getting Clear on Atheism, Agnosticism, and a Few Other Matters.* Houston Christian University.

https://hc.edu/news-and-events/2016/03/25/prove-god-exists/#:~:text=As%20mentioned%20earlier%2C%20evidence%20for,itself%20up%20to%20public%20scrutiny.

Corner, D. (ISSN 2161-0002). *Miracles.* Internet Encyclopedia of Philosophy.

https://iep.utm.edu/miracles/

Crabtree, V. (2007). *Natural Evil such as Earthquakes Evidence That God is Not Good.* The Human Truth Foundation.

http://www.vexen.co.uk/religion/theodicy_naturalevil.html

Craig, W. (1994). *Can a Loving God Send People to Hell? The Craig-Bradley Debate.* Reasonable Faith.

https://www.reasonablefaith.org/media/debates/can-a-loving-god-send-people-to-hell-the-craig-bradley-debate

Craig, W.L. (Eds.). (2015). *The Kalam Cosmological Argument.* Reasonable Faith.

https://www.reasonablefaith.org/writings/popular-writings/existence-nature-of-god/the-kalam-cosmological-argument

Craig, W.L. (2023). *The Problem of Miracles: A Historical and Philosophical Perspective.* Reasonable Faith.

https://www.reasonablefaith.org/writings/scholarly-writings/historical-jesus/the-problem-of-miracles-a-historical-and-philosophical-perspective

Craig, W.L. & Bradley, R. (Eds.) (1994). *Can a Loving God Send People to Hell? The Craig-Bradley Debate.* Reasonable Faith.

https://www.reasonablefaith.org/media/debates/can-a-loving-god-send-people-to-hell-the-craig-bradley-debate

Ebrahimi, H. et al. (2014). *The Effect of Spiritual and Religious Group Psychotherapy on Suicidal Ideation in Depressed Patients: A Randomized Clinical Trial.* The National Library of Medicine.

https://www.ncbi.nlm.nih.gov/pmc/articles/PMC4134174/

Eusebius., & Maier, P. (1999). *Eusebius: The Church History.* Kregel Publications.Fitzmyer, J. (1982). *The Gospel According to Luke.* Doubleday & Co.

Foley, A. & Lacey, T. (2014). *Supernatural or Science: How Do We Explain Miracles?* Answers in Genesis.

https://answersingenesis.org/apologetics/supernatural-or-science-how-do-we-explain-miracles/

Gaffin, R.(2023). *The Resurrection of Christ and Salvation.* The Gospel Coalition.

https://www.thegospelcoalition.org/essay/resurrection-christ-salvation/

Greear, J.D. (2015). *7 Truths about Hell.* TGC.

https://www.thegospelcoalition.org/article/7-truths-about-hell/

Griggs, J. (2023). *How Can a Loving God Send People to Hell?* Faith Hub.

https://faithhub.net/loving-god-people-hell-send/

Ham, K. (2014). *This is Why Everyone Should Believe in God.* Answers in Genesis.

https://www.youtube.com/watch?v=FF_6hWanmYw

HandWiki. (2022). *Historical Reliability of the Gospels.* Scholarly Community Encyclopedia.

https://encyclopedia.pub/entry/29465

Himma, K.E. (ISSN 2161-0002). *Anselm: Ontological Argument for the Existence of God.* Internet Encyclopedia of Philosophy.

https://iep.utm.edu/anselm-ontological-argument/

Holcomb, J. (2023). *What is the Proof and Evidence of the Resurrection of Jesus Christ?* Christianity.com.

https://www.christianity.com/jesus/death-and-resurrection/resurrection/what-proof-is-there-of-the-resurrection-of-jesus.html

Holcomb, J. (2014). *Why Don't We See Miracles Like The Apostles Did?* TGC.

https://www.thegospelcoalition.org/article/why-dont-we-see-miracles/

Howell, E. & Dobrijevic, D. (2022). *What is the Cosmic Microwave Background?* Space.com.

https://www.space.com/33892-cosmic-microwave-background.html

Jamison, S. (2021). *Showing Teenagers How Science Points to God as Creator.* Rooted Ministry.

https://rootedministry.com/teenagers-science-god-as-creator/

Jeremiah, D. (2023) *Why Does God Allow Suffering?* David Jeremiah Blog.

https://davidjeremiah.blog/why-does-god-allow-suffering/

King, H. (2018). *Bible Verses About How God Changes and Transforms Us.* Room to Breathe.

https://heathercking.org/2018/02/19/bible-verses-about-how-god-changes-and-transforms-us/

Lane, K. (2019) *Weekly Devotional: 4 Reasons to Trust God.* GCU.

https://www.gcu.edu/blog/spiritual-life/weekly-devotional-4-reasons-trust-god

Macy, H. (2011). *Community: God's Design for Growth.* Bible.org.

https://bible.org/article/community-god%E2%80%99s-design-growth

May, A. & Howell, E. (Eds.). (2023). *What is the Big Bang?* Space.com.

https://www.space.com/25126-big-bang-theory.html

McLatchie, J. (2020). *A Beginners Guide to the Kalam Cosmological Argument.* Solas.

https://www.solas-cpc.org/a-beginners-guide-to-the-kalam-cosmological-argument/

McRae, M. (2021). *Our Universe Is Finely Tuned for Life, and There's an Explanation for*

Why That Is So. ScienceAlert.

https://www.sciencealert.com/we-could-have-a-new-way-to-explain-why-our-universe-is-as-finely-tuned-for-life-as-it-is

Mental Models. *Entropy: The Hidden Force That Complicates Life.* Farnam Street.

https://fs.blog/entropy/

Minott, N. (Eds.) (2023). *5 Benefits of Faith.* RosemariesHeart.

https://rosemariesheart.com/blogs/faith/5-benefits-of-faith

Missler, C. (2023). *The Science of God.* Jesusonline. https://jesusonline.com/pvideothe-science-of-god-dr-chuck-missler/

Newberg, A. & Waldman, M.R. (2010). *How God Changes Our Brain: Breakthrough Findings From a Leading Neuroscientist.* Ballantine Books.

News. (2021). *Einstein believed in Spinoza's God. Who is That God?* Mind Matters. https://mindmatters.ai/2021/12/einstein-believed-in-spinozas-god-who-is-that-god/

Palau, L. (2004). *Five Ways God Answers Prayer.* Christianity Today. https://www.christianitytoday.com/biblestudies/articles/spiritualformation/five-ways-god-answers-prayer.html

Pecorino, P.A. (2001). *Chapter 3: Philosophy of Religion/ Proofs For The Existence of God/ The Problem of Evil.* StudyWeb, QCC. https://www.qcc.cuny.edu/socialsciences/ppecorino/intro_text/chapter%203%20religion/problem_of_evil.htm

Pecorino, P.A. (2001). *Philosophy of Religion: Chapter 6 - The Problem of Evil.* QCC. https://www.qcc.cuny.edu/socialsciences/ppecorino/phil_of_religion_text/CHAPTER_6_PROBLEM_of_EVIL/Nature_of_Evil.htm

Pecorino, P.A. (2001*). On Faith and Reason.* QCC. https://www.qcc.cuny.edu/socialsciences/ppecorino/phil_of_religion_text/CHAPTER_8_LANGUAGE/On-faith-and-reason.htm

Pecorino, P.A. (2001). *The Ontological Argument: Chapter 3 Philosophy of Religion.* QCC. https://www.qcc.cuny.edu/socialsciences/ppecorino/intro_text/Chapter%203%20Religion/Ontological.htm

Pecorino, P.A. (2001). *Relation of Faith to Reason, Section 4.* QCC. https://www.qcc.cuny.edu/socialsciences/ppecorino/phil_of_religion_text/CHAPTER_8_LANGUAGE/Relation_of_Faith_to%20Reason.htm

Perman, M. (2007). *Historic Evidence for the Resurrection.* Desiring God.

https://www.desiringgod.org/articles/historical-evidence-for-the-resurrection

Perman, M. (2023) *Understanding the Trinity: How can God be Three Persons in One?* CRU.

https://www.cru.org/us/en/train-and-grow/spiritual-growth/core-christian-beliefs/understanding-the-trinity.html

Piper, J. (2023). *Five Purposes for suffering.* Desiring God.

https://www.desiringgod.org/articles/five-purposes-for-suffering

Pomerleau, W.P. (ISSN 2161-0002). *Immanuel Kant: Philosophy of Religion.* Internet Encyclopedia of Philosophy.

https://iep.utm.edu/kant-rel/#:~:text=In%20a%20work%20published%20the,3

Price, R. & Eugene, OR. (Eds.). (1997). *The Stones Cry Out: What Archaeology Reveals About the Truth of the Bible.* Harvest House.

Ragland, C.P. (ISSN 2161-0002). *Hell.* The Internet Encyclopedia of Philosophy.

https://iep.utm.edu/hell/

Religious Studies. (2023). *The Nature of God.* BBC.

https://www.bbc.co.uk/bitesize/guides/zygbtv4/revision/8

Tacitus, C., Church, A.J. & Brodribb, W.J.,(Eds.). (1876). *The Annals, 15.44.* Wikisource.https://en.wikisource.org/wiki/The_Annals_(Tacitus)/Book_15

Schultz, V. (2018). *How Your DNA Points to Existence and Intricacy of God.* America The Jesuit Review.

https://www.americamagazine.org/faith/2018/02/01/how-your-dna-points-existence-and-intricacy-god

Tuggy, D. (ISSN 2161-0002). *Theories of Religious Diversity.* Internet Encyclopedia of Philosophy.

https://iep.utm.edu/reli-div/

Sharlow, M.F. (Eds.). (2009). *What's Really Wrong with the Argument from Design.* Philarchive.

https://philarchive.org/archive/SHAWRW#:~:text=Critics%20of%20the%20argument%20from,couldn't%20really%20be%20designed.

Simnowitz, A. (2013). *Son of God in the Old Testament.* The Journal of Biblical Missiology.

https://biblicalmissiology.org/blog/2013/02/11/son-of-god-in-the-old-testament/?gclid=Cj0KCQjw4s-kBhDqARIsAN-ipH17LgDWskAbjQHJsEN3Jl3aNsvLwgN52Xh619ZKRuOa5P5GoH0pimcaAhy-EALw_wcB

Slick, M. (2008). *Entropy and Causality Used as a Proof for God's Existence.* Carm.

https://carm.org/atheism/entropy-and-causality-used-as-a-proof-for-gods-existence/

Speaks, J. (2017-18). *Does God Exist? The Free Will Defense.*nd.edu.

https://www3.nd.edu/~jspeaks/courses/2017-18/10100/lectures/7-free-will-defense.pdf

Spector, N. (2018). *This Is Your Brain on Prayer and Meditation.* NBC News.

https://www.nbcnews.com/better/health/your-brain-prayer-meditation-ncna812376

Springer, J. (2023). *Intelligent Design: Can Science Answer, Does God Exist?* Life, Hope and Truth.

https://lifehopeandtruth.com/god/is-there-a-god/intelligent-design/

Staal, J. (2023). *Why Did God Give Us a Free Will?* Active Christianity.

https://activechristianity.org/why-did-god-give-us-a-free-will

Stewart, D. (2018). *Are the Four Gospels Historically Accurate?* Blue Letter Bible.

https://www.blueletterbible.org/Comm/stewart_don/faq/historical-accuracy-of-the-bible/question12-gospels-historically-accurate.cfm

Strobel, L. (1998). *The Case for Christ.* Zondervan.

Swindal, J. (ISSN 2161-0002). *Faith and Reason: Faith - Historical Perspectives.* Internet Encyclopedia of Philosophy.

https://iep.utm.edu/faith-re/

Tambagahan, S. (2023). *Five Types of Prayer.* The Word Community Church.

https://thewordfresno.org/five-types-of-prayer/

Taylor, P. (2011). *Did Miracles Really Happen?* Answers in Genesis.

https://answersingenesis.org/apologetics/did-miracles-really-happen/

The Life Team. (2023). *How did the Life of Jesus Impact the World?* The Life.

https://thelife.com/jesus-impact-the-world

Vassalos, L. (2018). *God's Existence: The* Wagner, P. (2019). *6 Reasons Why Worship Matters.* Church Leaders.

https://churchleaders.com/worship/worship-articles/161607-
philip_wagner_6_essential_reasons_why_worship_matters_worship.html

Waddle. J. (2022). *3 Consequences of Rejecting God's Authority (Psalm 2:1-2) Your Daily Bible Verse - October 24.* Crosswalk.com.

https://www.crosswalk.com/devotionals/your-daily-bible-verse/3-consequences-of-rejecting-god-s-authority-bible-study-minute-april-20-2018.html

Wallace, J. (2015). *Why the Information in our DNA Points to the Existence of God.* ColdCaseChristianity.

https://coldcasechristianity.com/writings/why-the-information-in-our-dna-points-to-the-existence-of-god/

Ware, B.A. (2023). *Mysticism, Rationalism, and Divine Revelation.* TGC.

https://www.thegospelcoalition.org/essay/mysticism-rationalism-and-divine-revelation/

Whitney, D. (2014). *A Description and Analysis of the Transcendental Argument for the Existence of God.* Morningview.

https://morningview.org/wp-content/uploads/2014/09/The-Transcendental-Argument-for-the-Existence-of-God-by-Tom-Hicks.pdf

Williams, D. (2023). *What Makes Christianity Different?* CRU.

https://www.cru.org/us/en/train-and-grow/spiritual-growth/core-christian-beliefs/what-makes-christianity-different.html

L.A. Buckley

Zukeran, P. (2008). *Historical Reliability of the Gospels.* Evidence and Answers.
https://evidenceandanswers.org/article/historical-reliability-of-the-gospels/

Bible Versions

Common English Bible

Contemporary English Version

English Standard Version

Good News Bible

New King James Version

New Living Translation

The Amplified Bible

The Living Translation

The Passion Translation